Mystics and Medics

A COMPARISON OF MYSTICAL AND PSYCHOTHERAPEUTIC ENCOUNTERS

Edited by
Reuven P. Bulka, Ph.D.

 **HUMAN SCIENCES PRESS**
72 Fifth Avenue   3 Henrietta Street
NEW YORK, NY 10011 ● LONDON, WC2E 8LU

This book is a revised and expanded version of *Mystics and Medics,* a special issue
of the *Journal of Psychology and Judaism.*   In altered form, it gathers essays which
appeared originally in that and other issues of the *Journal.*

Library of Congress Catalog Number 79-87593
ISBN: 0-87705-377-4
Copyright 1979 by Human Sciences Press

HUMAN SCIENCES PRESS
72 Fifth Avenue
New York, New York 10011

Printed in the United States of America

CONTENTS

INTRODUCTION

There is a lingering suspicion that the truths about human nature which have been uncovered in the last century are not new discoveries: rather they are insights into the human condition spelled out in the unique jargon of the psychology-language. If the observations of the twentieth century are valid, they are valid for all humankind spanning the generations. The truths of the twentieth century, if they are truths, are timeless.

The mystical world has, over the generations, taken a unique approach to the human situation. This approach has many psychological overtones. The present volume is concerned with the philosophical and meta-clinical encounters within mystical tradition and their similarities with modern clinical practice.

Zalman Schachter introduces the theme with an analysis of the transactional aspects of the Yehidut, the private encounter between hasid and master. In the process of this analysis, Schachter makes some interesting comparisons between the Yehidut and clinical encounter.

Jonathan Woocher explores the common ideas in the Kabbalah, Hasidism, and modern psychological thinking. He offers some fascinating points of common direction in those frameworks, although he makes it clear that mystical tradition and psychology have different ultimate objectives.

Judah Safier hones in on a specific element in the encounter, the paradox. He indicates the usages and value of paradox in the therapeutic setting and then shows how hasidic wisdom incorporated the energy of paradox in helping the hasid search for meaning.

Moshe HaLevi Spero, based on the articles by Woocher and Safier, attempts to distinguish between the hasid-rebbe encounter and the psychotherapeutic relationship, among other relationships. In spelling out the areas of life where they differ Spero at the same time suggests that the hasidic masters were, in fact, masters of human understanding.

Nathan Kuperstok, using the Chabad model, shows how Jewish mystical tradition facilitates the development of extended consciousness. Kuperstok does not deny that Judaism is concerned with the rational faculties; rather he posits a notion of wholeness which encompasses the left and right hemispheres of the brain.

James Kirsch explores some of the dreams of the famous hasidic sage, Rabbi Nachman of Bratzlav, employing Jungian notions. Kirsch's incisive analysis is a welcome counter to the reductionistic interpretations offered by others.

Jan Ehrenwald focuses on the mystique of prophecy and whether it shares common ground with precognition. Parapsychology is applied to an examination of the nature of prophecy, with the verdict of the modern laboratory inclining towards viewing Biblical prophecy as a unique and singular phenomenon inaccessible to scientific investigation.

In my concluding article, I have taken an unconventional approach to comparing hasidism and psychology. Hasidic anecdotes and aphorisms are projected parallel to counterparts in Frankl's logotherapy. The similarities between the two approaches are quite illuminating and understandable in terms of the common concern of hasidism and logotherapy to reorient distorted thinking.

Adding it all up, it is quite clear that the kabbalistic and hasidic traditions work in a different dimension from that of the modern clinic, but it is equally clear, at the same time, that kabbalistic and hasidic traditions have much to offer the modern clinician and philosopher.

Reuven P. Bulka

The Dynamics of the Yehidut Transaction

Zalman M. Schachter

The *yehidut* (literally, one-ing) may be described as a hasid's (disciple's) private encounter with his rebbe (master).

The yehidut is a transaction which is engaged in because one party—the hasid—has a need which the other party—the rebbe—can fill. From this simple description it might seem that the rebbe is the active party and the hasid is the passive one. This is not so. The hasid too must make his contribution to the yehidut. In other words, mutuality is essential to the transaction. The hasid must be prepared to give himself to the process of the yehidut. If he is not fully prepared to do so, the rebbe must help free him to participate fully in the transaction.

It is crucial to the yehidut transaction that each party—i.e., both rebbe and hasid—accept the other as he is. The hasid is prepared to accept the rebbe as "rebbe" because he has learned about him from others. But it is very difficult for the hasid to accept the rebbe as a person. The rebbe has fewer difficulties in accepting the hasid as a person; yet there are some qualifications to his acceptance of the hasid, and they are implicit in the relationship. The rebbe's acceptance of the hasid implies that both he and the hasid are included in the community whose sole pupose is to "do God's will with a perfect heart." Even if the person who comes to see the rebbe is unwilling to see himself as a member of this group, the rebbe will not permit his own motivation for involvement to slip from his awareness.

For the rebbe, acceptance of the person who comes for help, and the hope that he will become, if he is not already, a member of the hasidic God-serving community, go hand in hand; yet the latter is suppressed by the rebbe in favor of total acceptance. He is aware that the person seeking help may not be able to see himself in the role of a hasid. If he were to make this condition explicit, the seeker might not wish to continue the relationship, since he is, at this time, unwilling or unable to share the rebbe's value structure.

We have here a pedagogic formulation of acceptance that is temporarily satisfied with low-level extrinsic motives. Noble motives on the part of the hasid are the result and not the precondition of the rebbe's acceptance of the postulant. The love and acceptance of the rebbe for the postulant is predicated on the frankly persuasive principle which Abraham utilized with the strangers he fed (Schneerson, 1958). Because the task of education and guidance is to heal moral illnesses and to strengthen moral health (Schneerson, 1955), the rebbe cannot rely on the undivided help of the postulant, the one in need of strengthening in the transaction. He accepts that which seeks help in the hasid, as well as the tendency of the hasid to self-love, but only in order to circumvent it. The entire energy system of the transaction, on the parts of both rebbe and hasid, is one of love and empathy; and, in the same way as the rebbe would rid himself of all the destructive and evil characteristics were they his own, he is, for the sake of that love, committed to help the hasid eradicate them in himself.

II

"Thou shalt love thy neighbor as thyself, but not more than you love yourself," R. Schneur Zalman is reported to have said. "What you don't accept in your own self, you should not accept in your neighbor." In any candid transaction arising out of *ahavat Yisroel* (love of one's fellow Jew), there are two inclinations for good battling one inclination for evil, and the inclinations for good are sure to prevail.

This great love was celebrated by the Maggid of Mezeritch, who was heard to say that he wished he could love his own children as much as the Baal Shem Tov loved even the most wicked in Israel; and the love of the Maggid for his son, the Malach, was proverbial. R. Moshe Leib Sassov taught that one who could not with equanimity suck out the pus from another Jew's wound had not yet come to understand this love; and he explained how he was taught by two peasants at an inn that to love means to know what the other one lacks. No love of God is possible unless the love of Israel acts as the instrument for that love. The statements concerning the love of Israel could be multiplied many times. R. Abraham Yoshua Heschel of Apt wished to be known as the *Oheb Yisroel*—the lover of Israel. This he considered to be the supreme epitaph.

This great love energizes the rebbe-hasid relationship, and each experiences this energizing on his own level. The hasid sees in the yehidut the same mythic love experience that the rebbe celebrates for him in the description of the divine love. The *Tanya* teaches that if such a love as people share causes them to cleave to one another

> how much more so when a great and mighty king shows his great and intense love for a commoner who is despised and lowly among men, a disgraceful creature cast on the dunghill, yet he (the king) stoops down to him from the place of his glory, together with all his retinue, and raises him and exalts him from his dunghill and brings him into his palace, the royal palace, into the innermost chamber, a place such as no servant or lord ever enters; and there shares with him the closest companionship with embraces and kisses and spiritual attachment with all heart and soul—how much more will, of itself, be aroused a doubled and redoubled love in the heart of this most common and humble individual for the person of the king, with a true attachment of spirit, heart and soul, and with infinite heartfelt sincerity. Even if his heart be like a heart of stone, it will surely melt, and his soul will pour itself out like water, with soulful longing for the love of the king. (Schneur Zalman of Liadi, 1965a, p. 294)

The rabbis of the Talmud explain that the injunction "to fear the Lord your God" (*Deuteronomy,* 10:20) is intended to include the disciples of the wise (Talmud, *Pesahim,* 22b). The hasid applies this same equation to the injunction "to love the Lord your God" (*Deuteronomy,* 6:5), taking it to include the rebbe as well. If the rebbe is the head of the children of Israel (*Rosh B'nai Yisroel*—RBY), then the hasid is his limb, and the love and obedience of the limb for the head is boundless. The Habad principle, "the head rules the heart," becomes, by extension, the principle of the hasid's love and obedience to his rebbe. The guiding principle for the rebbe—*ahavat Yisroel*—is the vessel to *ahavat haShem*—the love of God. In other words, in the love of Israel is contained the love of God. The hasid's love for the rebbe is the sublimation of *ahavat Yisroel,* which is expressed when hasidim relate to one another, and follows the same direction as *ahavat haShem.* While the rebbe concretizes his love of God in his love for his hasidim, the hasid sublimates his love of God in his love for the rebbe.

We cannot discuss the love between rebbe and hasid without looking at the shadow side of their relationship. In the overt field of the relationship, all the polarities are contained, so that the basic Promethean rebellion in the hasid which is often unconsciously directed toward God is also directed toward the rebbe. All the father ambivalences are directed toward the rebbe. The hasid is glad for the paternal care, but at the same time angry that he needs it. The transference situation that applies in other helper-helped relationships and which manifests itself in both positive and negative terms, also applies here. This is not part of the hasid's general awareness and will not usually be raised by the rebbe to the level of conscious discussion. While the rebbe is generally more aware of his own negative transference than the hasid is of his, the rebbe clothes the negative feelings he may feel for the hasid in terms of annoyance over not being able to study Torah and pray at his leisure (Ze'ev Volf of Zhitomir, 1954).

The love which energizes the relationship between rebbe and hasid, and which, by its existence, makes possible the depth and scope of the yehidut, is atypical. This applies in comparison with other counselor-counselee relationships, as well as in comparison with other love relationships. In short, rebbe and hasid partake of a unique love relationship. Its uniqueness is largely a result of the fact that the love is not directed toward the manifest object of the love. The rebbe's love of God is manifested in his love for his hasid; the hasid's love of God is manifested in his love and devotion for the rebbe. The love relationship would not be possible were it not for the overpowering love of God which consumes both rebbe and hasid.

III

The rules of the rebbe-hasid transaction are implicit in the relationship. The hasid has heard how the rebbe, in discussing his own rebbe or ancestor, speaks of him as one who is "in the supernal model," an "absolute soul." He has heard that the "*rabbeyim* lived in the supernal image" (Schneerson, 1946, p. 5). Therefore, when he enters the yehidut, he knows that he stands before an archetypal model which is, in an essential way, completely inaccessible to him.

While remaining inaccessible himself, the rebbe makes the divine accessible to his hasid. Some of the hasid's life problems are rooted in his relationship with God; yet the hasid cannot work his problems out with God, at least not directly. And this is where the rebbe, as an archetypal model, serves the hasid. He functions as a conjunctive person; he responds to the hasid's problem by answering, scolding, and even by giving the needed pat on the back.

The conjunctive function of the rebbe is of great importance in the transaction between rebbe and hasid. Against the "divine" role which the rebbe assumes, the hasid can work out his problems with some assurance of definite results. When the rebbe assures him of children and health, the hasid knows that the rebbe, like Moses, is the mouthpiece of God, and that "the Divine Presence speaks through the throat of Moses" (Hayman, 1955, p. 524). If the rebbe were not there to mediate the divine, the covenantal relationship between the hasid and God would not be concretized. None of the accessible means of communion with God are equal to the mediation of the rebbe. In the presence of the rebbe, and in the demands he makes on his life, God becomes real for the hasid. The rebbe stands, as it were, in *loco dei,* and his pronouncements are of fiatic character.

As the archetypal model, the rebbe serves not only the hasid's being, but also his becoming. He is the human archetype as well as the divine one, and as such, he represents to the hasid the potential of his own becoming. As a human archetype, the rebbe gives direction to the hasid's striving.

In order to establish the rebbe's authority, Hasidism must place him hierarchically above the hasid. Yet in order to maintain his effectiveness, the rebbe cannot be too far beyond the reach of the hasid. While he may have become the most exalted personage, he must have started from the lowest rung in order that hasidim can learn from him. The functional tension between the rebbe's exaltedness and his popular involvement is always present. A rebbe will state that it was hard work and not an exalted soul which brought him to present station. But his hasid, in order to defend himself from the rebbe's challenge, places him back on the pedestal. The rebbe's reminder, "You need not think that a rebbe is that much greater than you—it is enough if you think him a handsbreadth higher" (Mordecai of Lekhovitz et al., 1961, p. 240), is accompanied by the hasid's rejoinder that this handsbreadth is qualitatively impassable.

This attitude is not only the defense of the aspirant, but also the defense of the community in which he lives. The hasidic community must not let a hasid escape its own plane of being. If he succeeds in ascending beyond their range, he is a challenge to them, and they will have to invoke a rationale for his escape from earthboundness. In order to do this, they will speak of the exalted level of his soul. If he becomes a rebbe after his master's demise, it only serves to prove the community's case that he was not an ordinary soul to begin with. If one were to point to an aspirant's humble beginnings, the community would merely reply: "it sometimes happens that the soul of an infinitely lofty person enters to become the son of a despised and lowly man" (Schneur Zalman of Liadi, 1965a, p. 30).

All the possibilities are covered in order that the rebbe's accessibility as a model does not become too great a source of anxiety for the individual hasid or for the community. At times the rebbe, for reasons of his own, collaborates with this attitude. He may do this because he does not want his hasid to suffer undue anxiety, or because he does not want the hasid to aspire to heights that are beyond his present reach. Or, the rebbe may do this simply because he wishes to foster Zaddikism.

Although the hasid may never aspire to copy the rebbe in his inner being—this he considers too remote—he is expected to copy certain aspects of the rebbe's behavior. The fact that the rebbe does not afford the hasid much access to his own inner life reinforces the attitude that the rebbe's speech and actions, at least on some levels, may serve as accessible models, but not his inner life. In this vein the Lechvitzer replied to his son's question as to whether the hasidic masters belonged among the thirty-six hidden saints by saying: "Child, what kind of a face would we have if all that were to our being would be what is manifest?" (Kleinman, 1958, p. 5).

Or, after the Ziditchover once enumerated his rungs, the Ropshitzer exclaimed to the Apter: "What humility! He mentioned only the very lowest ones" (Berger, 1906/1954, p. 19).

In spite of the implicit understanding that only the rebbe's manifest behavior is accessible to the hasid, there are exceptions. Where a hasid aspires to greater discipleship, the rebbe's inner life may be made accessible to him.

Whenever the rebbe acts specifically as rebbe, the hasid must not even emulate his behavior. Whenever the rebbe acts as an exalted "servant of God," the disciple may venture to emulate him. Generally, the hasid remains in the posture of adulation, seeing in the rebbe a person who points in the direction of the service he must render to God. Whenever the rebbe acts as a hasid, he is the model of hasidic etiquette and custom, and a hasid must not venture beyond the modes of behavior set by the rebbe's own behavior. In this way, the rebbe creates and formulates the hasidic wont.

Where conscious copying is suspected, hasidim react adversely. The more unconscious the copying, the higher the moral rating.

The rebbe who looks at a hasid as he enters the yehidut can gauge his level of adherence to the hasidic wont by his clothes and behavior. It may serve as a visible index of the hasid's willingness to follow the rebbe's advice.

The rebbe's function as a model for the hasid is implicit in the yehidut transaction. The hasid, in relating to the rebbe, is aware of the areas of accessibility and non-accessibility and responds accordingly. The rebbe's partial accessibility is both a challenge and a cause for anxiety. It challenges him in his becoming, while, at the same time, making him anxious over the great gulf between his achievement and that of the rebbe. The rare hasid who truly responds to the challenge will become a disciple. By and large, hasidim will minimize the rebbe's accessibility in order to decrease their own anxiety.

As an archetypal model, the rebbe acts in a conjunctive role. He mediates the divine to the hasid, thus concretizing the hasid's relationship with God. God becomes real to the hasid through his relationship with the rebbe.

IV

The hasid comes to the rebbe with high aims and often the rebbe feels chastised by the hasid and the purity of his aspirations. The hasid's highest soul level, that of his "delight and will," which is located in his *yehidah* (the highest state of the soul), has great significance in the yehidut. The rebbe must meet the hasid by locating the lowest of his own levels lower than the highest of the hasid's levels. This creates a disparity. The hasid's "ought" reaches higher than the rebbe's "is," and serves as an inspiration to the rebbe.

Many rebbes have confessed that they needed their hasidim for inspiration. Often a hasid's simple concern for another becomes a rebbe's inspiration. The rebbe is always on the lookout for good points in his hasidim which may be used for intercession to effect salutary benefits for the entire community of Israel and for individuals in need of help.

The rebbe sees, in each individual who comes to him to seek his help, the possibility of a new insight.

Once R. Shalom of Belz sat at the table (*tish*) and a woman came and wept before him about her plight of barrenness and begged his blessing to conceive. The rebbe blessed her and she went. The rebbe sat for a while, lost in meditation. Then, turning to his hasidim, he said: "You saw this woman. She has already come several times, and each time I blessed her. Yet she came again. So I bethought myself: "She comes to me, and all I am is flesh and blood; yet she continues to come. How much more ought we to come and place our requests before Him Who is the

King of Kings!" Out of this meditation did I also beg for her. And with
God's help she was blessed with children. (Klopholtz, 1965, vol. 2, p. 252)

Even the proverbial "nudnik," the unlettered one who interrupts the
tish, has a positive value for the rebbe, as the following story illustrates:

> Rabbi Levi Yitzhak often welcomed at his table an honest and untaught
> man whom his disciples regarded askance because they thought him
> incapable of understanding what the rabbi said. And what business has
> one who boils pitch among those who compound ointments! But because
> the man was good-natured and simple, he either did not notice the at-
> titude of the rabbi's disciples, or did not let it ruffle him, so that finally
> they asked the zaddik's wife to show the lout the door. Since she did not
> want to do this without her husband's permission, she reported to him
> the misgivings and the request of his disciples. The rabbi replied: "When
> the Seven Shepherds once sit at the holy feast: Adam, Seth, Methuselah
> to the right, Abraham, Jacob, Moses to the left, David in the middle, and
> a poor untutored man, Levi Yitzhak of Berditchev, goes up to them, I
> believe they will even nod to that lout." (Buber, 1948, p. 221)

Thus, even the simplest hasid teaches the rebbe something. Yet, the
more complex the hasid is, the greater will be the rebbe's involvement
with him, since it occurs on many more levels.

V

When interacting with his hasid, the rebbe must integrate the various factors of the hasid's make-up: divine, animal and rational souls,
temperament and constitution, present and past lives.
The rebbe who meets a hasid who has fallen back from the straight
and narrow path, will ask him: "Where are you?" This question,
"Ayeko?," which God asked of Adam, has perennial reverberations in
the hasidic universe. The hasid who came to Kotzk and was asked by
the rebbe, "From where?," felt challenged to the quick. The rebbe confronted the hasid in this abrupt manner in order to have him choose
one of his selves for the sake of the interview.
The rebbe cannot transact anything of real significance if he deals
only with the hasid's pious self and not with the self in him that makes
the real decisions. If the two selves happen to be identical, there is no
problem in the transaction. The rebbe, however, knows that there are
very few who act as authentic selves. In hasidic parlance, a person
who—under God—is fully autonomous, is referred to as an *azmi,* an

absolute self. In speaking of his father, the late Lubavitcher rebbe referred to him as an *azmi*. A hasid will be flattered if the rebbe refers to him as a *p'nimi*, an interior person. The *p'nimi* acts out of deep inner compunction; he is never fickle. A contract made with an *azmi* is the most serious one. The worst contract is one made with a hypocrite. Among hasidim he was outside the pale. But a close neighbor was the *hizon* (emotionally shallow person), the opposite of the *p'nimi*. He was considered capable of emotions which he readily showed, but which were shallow and did not commit him to any action.

A yehidut with a *hizon* was very difficult since the immediacy of his response soon vanished because it was momentarily sincere, but shallow. The rebbe, receiving the appropriate response from a *hizon*, could be sure only of the *hizon's* ease of responding, but not of any appreciable change in his life. In order for the *hizon* to become a hasid with whom the rebbe could transact significantly, the rebbe would first have to produce in him a greater depth and a larger inner life. Even in a person who was closer to a *p'nimi* than a *hizon*, the rebbe had to establish contact with the "manager" of the person.

The teachings of Habad were directed toward the *beynoni*, the man who is managed by his rational soul. A contract with the divine soul, which obligated the *beynoni* at Sinai, and to which he was adjured at birth, was one that only the divine soul, and not the whole person, would honor. There is no point in attempting a transaction with the animal soul, since it is bent on seeking only its own pleasures. The only real contractual partner is the rational soul. Neither the divine soul nor the animal soul can force behavior. All behavior is the function of the go-ahead signal of the rational soul.

Yet the rational soul experiences problems of its own in dealing with identities and roles. The father role in a person differs from the husband role, and both roles differ from those of the merchant and the hasid. When the hasid faces the rebbe, he faces him as "hasid," but, on the level of his problem, he may be another person. A hasid who was unhappily married wanted to ask the rebbe about the advisability of a divorce. Several times he came to the rebbe, and each time, the hasid in him monopolized the conversation. He had to return yet another time, and this time the rebbe recognized that he was now dealing with another person and dealt immediately with the matter of the divorce.

The rebbe has to meet many of the hasid's levels. In order to do this, he must reveal several levels of his own being. This he does by showing a genuine interest in the worldly affairs of the hasid.

The rebbe must deal not only with the many sides of a hasid's own being, but also with the many significant persons the hasid has introjected. When a young hasid came to the rebbe about a problem which the rebbe knew was not his own, the rebbe asked that he send his *mashpiya* (guide) to him. The rebbe then berated the *mashpiya* for burdening the hasid with his own problem. Here we are not dealing with a genuine case of introjection. The young man had been coached for his yehidut, and the *mashpiya* had projected. The rebbe was able to discern this projection.

Parental vestiges in the hasid are not so easily dealt with since the hasid may be unaware of their existence. Another reason is that the rebbe will not wish to remove these parental vestiges completely since they are often of great help to the hasid. The hasid could not say "My God and God of my fathers" if he did not have a good parental deposit in himself. What is important here is that the rebbe separate the hasid from his parental introjections if they interfere with his progress.

The interaction of the rebbe with parental or other influences can often be dealt with in a more direct manner. The rebbe may report to the hasid that he has spoken with the discarnate soul of the father or any other ancestor and has gotten him to agree to the counsel he is about to give the hasid. That the rebbe can do so is not questioned by the hasid. Hasidim are familiar with many such stories. A story is told, for example, of how the soul of the Ari appeared to the Baal Shem Tov and they argued over an interpretation of Torah. The Ari finally agreed to the Baal Shem Tov's interpretation (Buber, 1948, p. 75).

Parental introjections are not the only introjections with which a rebbe may have to deal. Each hasid may have his own introjections which present a problem in the rebbe-hasid transaction. Occasionally a hasid may decide, for reasons of his own, to change rebbes. This is a rare occurrence, and when it happens, the hasid usually fears the wrath of his former rebbe. In this case, he will seek the protection of his new rebbe. But his problem may not be that simple. In all probability, he will have incorporated many of the values of his former rebbe, and these may be a hindrance to him in his relationship with his present rebbe. Thus, the rebbe will first have to deal with these assumed values before a meaningful transaction can ensue.

In addition to dealing with the hasid's many selves, the rebbe is aware of the fact that he must take on the hasid's dark side if he is to help him. The hasid may have committed a considerable number of sins, and each sin has brought him deeper into the realm of *k'lipah* (evil). The rebbe must protect the hasid from the onslaughts of this realm. By personifying the hasid's sins in terms of evil entities, the rebbe faces the demonic aspects of the hasid. He must wrestle with the hasid's vices which are not always readily accessible to his help (Mordecai of Lekhovitz et al., 1961, p. 241).

The rebbe must also interact with the hasid in the transcendental realm. The rebbe must open for the hasid such gates and channels as the hasid needs to have opened for him. If the hasid is in need of healing, the rebbe has to seek healing for him from the realm of health. At times, the rebbe may find his path blocked. In such a case, he will have to open a channel for the hasid by devious means. A hasid who suffered from a fatal disease traveled from master to master and gained no help until he came to R. Pinhas of Koretz, who wished him great wealth. The rebbe later explained that while he found the gates of health blocked to him, he was able to open the gates of other abundance to the hasid, and once he had achieved this, he was able to gain for the hasid a new lease on life.

VI

The rebbe's involvement with his hasid commits him to interact not only with the hasid's present, but also with his past and future. His empathy must therefore include both the hasid's being—a composite of his past and present—and his becoming, his movement toward his future. To understand the hasid's problematic being, the rebbe must be able to view him "in situation;" he must be able to see him as a particular person with a particular problem. To see either the hasid or his problem in isolation would be to get only a distorted view.

The rebbe sees the hasid's problem in terms of process. In the process of life, there are many moments of crisis.

> Especially since man is called "mobile" and not "static," he must ascend from level to level and not remain forever at one plateau. Between one level and the next, before he can reach the higher one, he is in a state of decline from the previous level. Yet, it is written, "Though he falls, he shall not be utterly cast down." It is considered a decline only in comparison with his former state, and not, G-d forbid, in comparison with all other men, for he is still above them in his service (of G-d), inasmuch as there remains in it an impression of his former state. (Schneur Zalman of Liadi, 1965b, pp. 9–10)

The hasid experiences a "death" in his need to regress from his former level and being. This is part of his grooming for the next level. Yet at the moment of his fall, he feels that he is forever arrested on this fallen level, and comes to the rebbe in the desperation of his plight. At this point, the rebbe must utilize his empathy in order to ask himself what it feels like to be forever arrested at this particular stage, and to feel that the predicament is a permanent one. He must be able to fully feel the hopelessness and despair which the hasid feels, yet he must not allow the hasid to give way to his feeling of despair. The rebbe knows that the hasid's condition is not permanent, for he knows that "man is judged every day," and this means that tomorrow will be a different day and a different judgment.

Once the Baal Shem Tov's disciples asked him concerning the contradiction between "man's budget is granted to him from Rosh Hashanah to Rosh Hashanah" and "man is judged every day." The rebbe replied by knocking on the window and calling the water-carrier, Yuckel. "Yuckel, tell me how are you today?" the Baal Shem Tov asked. "Oy rebbe," Yuckel replied, "I am old and my shoulders are weak; and the children are studying Torah and not one thinks of helping me. My wife is old and sickly, and my sons-in-law conduct themselves like rabbis, and all that on my shoulders, rebbe. I don't want to sin, but I feel depressed by all my woes."

The next day the Baal Shem Tov called him again, and again he asked him "How do you feel today?" Yuckel chuckled and said, "Rebbe, you know I am a lucky man. I have fine children, and sons-in-law who study Torah, and my wife, she is such a darling and keeps house well, despite her being old and sickly; and to think of it—all this is borne on these old shoulders! Yes rebbe, I am a lucky man. May God be praised for His abundant graces."

After the Baal Shem Tov dismissed Yuckel, he turned to his disciples and said, "See, not a single thing has changed. Yuckel is the same and his budget unvarying, but today he was judged differently."

By dealing with his hasid in this manner, the rebbe plots him on a course; he helps the hasid to see himself as part of a process, rather than as a static being. In this way, he can be assured that what seems terrible and impossible one day, may find its resolution the next. The hasid's problem is but a station on the way.

The rebbe faces the hasid in three ways, but these ways are not mutually separable. Each is an intertwining thread in the ongoing being of the hasid. The rebbe faces the hasid in his manifest being as a person in trouble; he faces him in his interactions with his own many selves; and he faces him in the dynamics of his becoming. But the rebbe also faces the hasid simultaneously in another dimension. This dimension is a divine ontological moment; it is the way in which a soul stands in the primeval thought of *Adam Kadmon* (primeval man—man in God's conception). It is a moment in which this particular life has achieved its specific destiny, although the momentum of the dynamics of becoming will not allow the soul to hold on to this moment. At this ontic moment, that soul's particular plan and destiny is worked out as it stood in the primal thought. As Agnon put it:

A person has three beings. The first being is the way in which a person perceives himself, the second is the way in which a person is seen by others, and the third being is prior to the first, and it is the being by which he was created by Him who created him. If a person merited and did not damage the being which his Creator made him, then that being overwhelms the other two, and then even his shadow inspires grace and beauty. (Agnon, 1975, p. 263)

The third being is the soul as it stands in the primal thought. The rebbe, then, must be able to interact with the hasid in the dimension of this moment which has ongoing significance. To interact on this level Viktor Frankl considers "the finest maxim for any kind of psychotherapy," and here he quotes Goethe:

When we take man as he is, we make him worse; but when we take man as if he were already what he should be, we promote him to what he can be. (Frankl, 1968, p. 18)

The rebbe is therefore involved in a cross tug of tensions which operate in at least two dimensions: (a) the tension between total identification and objectivity; and (b) the tension between the hasid's problem as a vexing static condition and as a point in the hasid's dynamic movement. Or, to put it in more traditional, hasidic terms—the tension is between the goals and purposes of this incarnation in which the problem brought to the rebbe occurs, and the goals and purposes of the person's reincarnational life in which the problem figures as a point on a curve. The rebbe's manifold tensions in feeling the problem with the hasid are also the dimensions of his creativity in helping the hasid.

Another important function of the rebbe's interaction with his hasid lies in arrangement making. Arrangement making refers to a restructuring of the sequence of the hasid's loyalties, responsibilities and priorities. The purpose of this restructuring is to free the hasid from a cross-tug of tensions which holds him at dead center. The arrangement need not represent a final action directive for the hasid; it is enough that it act in such a way as to divert the tensions which are restricting the hasid's movement. The hasid may require help in making a series of progressive rearrangements, each one freeing him for the next task. Arrangement making is thus a temporary restructuring which serves the purpose of freeing the hasid from tensions which are crippling his movement.

The ruse of arrangement making is often necessary because the person in need of help is unable to shift his precarious economy by himself. The arrangement of his defenses is set in such a fashion that the slightest move on his part seems to topple the entire economic structure of his psyche. The rebbe's first move is to help the hasid shore up his defenses. This he does by distracting him from his present position, where, at tremendous cost to his psychic economy, he must guard and protect all possibilities. Here the rebbe's task is not as difficult as that of other helpers in the same position. The hasidic structure enables the rebbe to call upon the hasid's faith in him. Because he is able to demand this trust on the part of the hasid, the rebbe can more easily deflect him from his care and anxiety. In placing himself in the rebbe's hands, the hasid is able to let down his defenses because he trusts that the rebbe will protect him. Any insight which the hasid may gain from seeing his problems restructured in such a way will provide only a temporary framework for movement.

This framework will, in all probability, have to undergo a process of several adjustments until a clear "objective" insight, to replace all the temporary insights, is reached. Each adjustment is a step in a series of distractions whose object is to bring the hasid to the point where he is able to act without tension on the instruction that the rebbe wished to give him in the first place.

The process we have described is the one referred to by R. Nachman in his discussion of the method of helping those weaker souls whom he called "eggs" (1960, p. 75). He explained that because their outer protection is so weak, it can easily crack. Figuratively speaking, such "eggs" have both a rounded and a pointed end, the rounded end representing insensitivity, and the pointed end representing sensitivity. In order to help such a soul, the rebbe must be able to "turn" him so that his "sharp end" will be directed toward those areas in which sensitivity has positive value, and his "round end" will be directed toward those areas in which sensitivity is undesirable. Since it is not advisable to turn such souls all at once, the rebbe must do so gradually.

This method of arrangement making is based on Maimonides' (1967) Theory of Education which proceeds from lesser values to higher values by providing an ever-ascending scale of values. The rebbe's ability to assist his hasid in a gradual ascending movement is part of his understanding of the hasid's life process.

The disciple engages in yehidut because he believes the rebbe can fill his need. Though they interact on many levels, the rebbe cannot diagnose by external and mechanical methods. He uses no questionnaire, no projective tests. He is the diagnostic instrument, the one who reads the scales, integrates the readings, and plans a course of help. Yet, being human, he is subject to the human condition. He is affected by what he sees, and this can cause distortions. In order to be an effective helper, the rebbe has to know how to transcend his human condition. This can only be done by constant effort and vigilance.

"Investment" is the literal translation of the hasidic term *hitlabshut*. Figuratively, the term expresses the rebbe's action in clothing himself in the garments of the hasid's thought, word, and deed. These he examines from within, thus fulfilling the command, "Do not judge a fellow until you have arrived at that fellow's place" (Talmud, *Aboth,* 2:4). The rebbe takes this command literally. He assumes the place of the hasid and enters his consciousness, while at the same time retaining his hold on his own consciousness.

VII

Imagine a person who has been treated surgically, and is asked how the treated part of the anatomy feels. Let us assume that it was the foot that was treated. In order to answer the question meaningfully, the patient must become "all foot." If the patient remained "all head," the patient could not really answer the question about the foot. Yet, at the same time, the patient must bring the feeling of the foot to the attention of the head. If one is to do something about the foot, one cannot consult the foot about the course of action, but must consult the head. Still, a decapitated head cannot answer the question about the foot.

According to the hasidic view, the rebbe is the Head of the People. He feels what they feel. He is the head and can advise the foot about the proper remedy.

The field of interaction between rebbe and hasid coheres because they are bound to one another in a relationship which is known as *hitkashrut* (commitment to a rebbe). In the yehidut, *hitkashrut* becomes more intense and profound, and *hitlabshut*—investment— enters the picture. In *hitkashrut,* the hasid remains hasid, and the rebbe remains rebbe. In *hitlabshut,* the rebbe becomes the hasid for the moment. *Hitlabshut* is more than trial identification. The rebbe has already received the *quittel* (written request), and in the process of *hitlabshut* he sees the hasid in his abiding and recurring personal essence. *Hitlabshut* provides the rebbe with a basic area of empathy and understanding. From here, he can proceed to establish the external information he needs in order to help his hasid. This field of empathy enables the rebbe to experience the hasid's problem on a subtle level within himself.

When the men of our convenant enter into yehidut and reveal the things that plague their hearts in their innermost being, each one according to his state, then each thing they tell me I must find in myself in its subtle form, or in the subtle form of the subtle form. It is impossible to answer

him and give him something to mend his ways and truly order his life
until one mend this matter first in oneself, and only then can one give an
ezah and a tikun. (Schneerson, 1935, Kuntres 30, p. 3)

The process of investment is very debilitating for a rebbe who must
interview a large number of hasidim each day. "Yehidut is very expensive in health," one rebbe explained, because

Yehidut is a continuing investment and divestment. . . .the investment of
becoming the other and the divestment in order not to be the other any
more, but to invest himself in the next one, is a great psychic exertion.
(Schneerson, 1947, p. 20)

The burden of the rebbe is great. Since the rebbe participates in the
hasid's world view, he sees the hasid's problems in terms of evil decrees
which have to be removed, rigors of law that have to be sweetened at
their root. The rebbe cannot simply tell the hasid that he must learn to
live with his problem. Even if this is necessary because there is no
immediate solution available at the root of the hasid's soul, the rebbe
still has to reach much higher. He must reach into a previous incarnation of the hasid in order to show him why he must live with his
problems now because of their reparative value.

What is that element which provides for the identification of rebbe
with hasid? It is obvious that here one is not dealing with objective
problem solving. The rebbe has to feel in himself the pain of his hasid.
Where the natural impulse of one who is in his position might be to
laugh at the hasid's problem, which, viewed from a vertical perspective, might seem insignificant, the rebbe, through the process of his
identification with the hasid, will sigh at the hasid's agony. The rebbe
is able to fully identify with his hasid because, at the moment when he
gives the hasid his undivided attention, he is also giving his undivided
attention to God, and the one makes possible the other. This paradox is
difficult for the modern reader to comprehend, yet there are many
hasidic tales which illustrate just this point.

R. Naphtali of Ropshitz, who was very fond of joking and punning, one
day, in his later years, decided that he was not going to talk anymore.
His family was very much upset: they addressed him, but they would
receive no answer from him. Finally, they sent his son, R. Eliezer of
Dzhikov, to see what was wrong with his father. R. Naphtali explained:
"At one time I was able to keep two things in my mind at the same time. I
would joke with a person, while, at the same time, intending to some very
high unifications in the mind of God. Now that I am old, and am able to
think only one thought at a time, I do not want to talk, because to talk
would mean that I cannot be in the presence of God." (Berger, 1906/1954,
p. 86)

Even a latter-day rebbe, R. Kalonymos Kalmish of Piasetzno, was once asked if his great involvement with his hasidim did not prevent him from pursuing his work. R. Kalonymos, by way of reply, pointed to a pad on his desk on which he had marked down some deep kabbalistic insights. He explained that every time one of his hasidim left his presence, he tried to understand the hasid's problem in terms of a kabbalistic problem, and the solution that he offered was in terms of a solution to the problem in kabbalah. In this way, he managed to be active in his own vineyard, writing and studying, while at the same time tending the vineyards of his hasidim (Shapira, 1960).

This illustration emphasizes the belief held by the rebbe concerning problems brought to him by his hasidim. He believes that every problem is a special message from God. This fact enables him to learn at the same time as he is helping his hasid. This means that he is not merely passing the hasid's problems into a previously established gestalt.

One of the most difficult problems of the rebbe—R. Shmuel of Lubavitch considered it the most difficult, is the fact that he must continually invest and divest himself so completely that there will be no transfer of person or problems from one hasid to the next. Often rebbes would use the moments in between *yehidot* for intercession in order to remove any incubatory element from their conscious mind. Thus, they would be able to meet the situation of the next hasid in terms of its own structure.

VIII

In order to bring the relevant material of Hasidism to bear on the process of investment and divestment, it is useful to digress to the process of empathy as discussed by Katz, and employing Reik's outline of the process of empathy. This process may occur in the following order: 1. identification; 2. incorporation; 3. reverberation; and 4. detachment. It is possible that the order may change, or—and this is more often the case in the psychological realm—the phases may occur simultaneously.

Presumably, the rebbe is a master of the empathetic process. Since too much awareness of the process may inhibit the engagement of emotion in the other (Katz, 1963, p. 41), the rebbe will deliberately regress since he trusts his empathy. Yet he is not anxious over his need to regress since he trusts the "unconscious *ruach hakodesh*" (holy spirit) to help him maintain the proper frame of mind to be able to detach himself when necessary.

In order to lose his "objectiveness," the rebbe calls on his experience so that he may discover the hasid's problem on a subtle level in himself. To compare again with Katz:

> Only when we detect something familiar in our own experience, do we appreciate the quality of the other's experience which we have internalized. "I personally feel I only 'understand' if I can detect in my own mind the germ of a similar feeling as the one which I try to understand, given that a similar thing should happen to me." (Katz, 1963, p. 45)

Hasidism, at its inception, was erroneously identified with Sabbatianism. In the Sabbatian, and in many other gnostic systems, one must *actually* experience the experience of the other. The rebbe, on the other hand, knows that this is not necessary. If it were, the whole helping process would place the helper in terrible jeopardy. All that is necessary is that the helper find the same problem in himself on "a subtle level." Discussing this from the angle of empathy, Katz explains that

> It is not essential that we experience the actual event. We can imagine the event and anticipate what our own response might be. *We have within ourselves the potentialities of every human response. Because we share this common emotional endowment, we are able to understand from within ourselves what the meaning of the experience of others might be for them.* We could not recognize the other's experience unless we had some *a priori* knowledge of it. (1963, p. 45)

Hasidism has its system of correspondences and its system of the evolution of the higher cause down to the lower effect. Since the zaddik can be held responsible for the sins of his generation (*Deuteronomy Rabbah,* 1:13), it is understandable that the experience of the body follows the more subtle experience of the head. On the subtle level, the rebbe has had the same experience, and he must find it and raise it to the conscious level. If he is unable to raise it to consciousness, he will fear that he is repressing his subtle involvement, and that it may be evil that is hidden in the depth of the depths (Schneerson, 1935).

The rebbe's subtle experience is both the same and not the same as that of the hasid. To the rebbe, his subtle experience has the same meaning as the hasid's gross experience has to him. In the hasidic system, the rebbe's subtle experience contains the hasid's gross experience as cause contains effect. Therefore, as far as hasidic ontology is concerned, the rebbe's experience is not merely symbolic, rather it is identical with the hasid's own experience.

Despite the fact that this is an expensive process in terms of health and emotions on the part of the rebbe, the rebbe gains a great deal in the form of his own perfection. The hasid stimulates the rebbe and enriches the rebbe's scope. The rebbe lacks some experiences in his own life. When the hasid brings his problems to the rebbe, and the rebbe invests himself in them, he empathetically experiences the hasid's life. Had the hasid not brought his problems to the rebbe, the rebbe would not have had occasion to plumb the depths of his range of subtle experience.

The rebbe's investment in his hasidim is reinforced on a depth level by the fact that he makes his living from the honoraria which his hasidim provide. The rebbe must protect his investment in his hasid, and his hasid's investment in him. This is the significance of the *pidyon* (ransom) for the rebbe. The *pidyon* is a retainer, and the rebbe must act as an agent retained by a client.

IX

The rebbe's investment in the hasid is facilitated by the fact of the hasid's investment in his rebbe. According to custom, the hasid who comes to yehidut has already heard the rebbe's discourses, and has made the concepts and values discussed in them his own. While these may not yet be fully internalized working parts of the hasid's consciousness, they are nevertheless part of his upward strivings.

Just as the rebbe experiences difficulties in his investment in and empathy with his hasid, even more so does the hasid experience difficulties in his investment. In coming to the yehidut, the hasid may so absorb the atmosphere of the rebbe's court before his interview, and may so empathize with the rebbe during the yehidut, that he sees himself as he supposes the rebbe sees him.

Thus, the image which the hasid will have of himself will be neither that which he normally sees as himself, nor that which the rebbe sees him as, but rather a fictitious image which is a product of the hasid's own mind under the environmental influences which exist. Such an image can be a block to the productive interaction between rebbe and hasid. R. Mendel of Kotzk, concerned about this phenomenon, taught the following maxim:

> If I am I because you are you, and you are you because I am I, then you are not you and I am not I. But, if I am I because I am I, and you are you because you are you, then I am I and you are you and we can talk. (Buber, 1948, p. 283)

Whatever good the hasid will derive from the yehidut must arise from an authentic interrelation with the rebbe.

In Chabad Hasidism, this interaction is seen in terms of the rebbe's lower level descending below the hasid's higher level. Thus the relationship is established. The hasid's strivings, the level of the *yehidah* (highest state) of his soul, where his capacity for delight and the power of his will reside, reach upward toward the rebbe, and even higher into the Divine Will. The rebbe, on the other hand, by the power of the *yehidah* soul level, can descend even to the lowest levels and yet remain fully aware on the highest level of awareness. Both of these *yehidah* movements—upwards and downwards—are aspects of *m'sirat nefesh*—self sacrifice. The hasid is prepared to change his entire mode of life, and the rebbe is prepared to descend into the hasid's private hell.

X

The rebbe knows that his efforts at revealing secrets to his hasid may cost him the lives of his own children; yet he also knows that he cannot do anything but act in the way he must, since this is the purpose of his existence (Sternhartz, p. 150).

At the moment when he must invest himself most deeply in his hasid, the rebbe experiences a temptation to escape this involvement and settle down to solitary study and prayer. But he has been told by his own master that his involvement with his hasid is in the service of his own life. If the rebbe fulfills his own task too soon, he may have to die as there will no longer be any purpose for his life on earth (Klopholtz, 1965, p. 211). Thus, the hasid distracts the rebbe from his thirst to become lost in God, and in this way, keeps him alive (Berger, 1906/1954, p. 90).

The rebbe, having allowed himself to become aware of his hasid's attitude toward him, is bound to the relationship. Awareness and empathy cause positive feedback, and this increases the mutual empathy. The hasid relates to the rebbe more fully, and the hasid's empathizing with the rebbe stimulates the rebbe to invest himself ever more deeply into the hasid.

It is almost as if the rebbe acted against his better judgment. Each time he opens himself to the hasid, he opens himself to pain. "I feel his pain even more than he does," R. Nachman of Bratzlav said of one hasid. "He can at least become distracted from his pain, but I cannot" (Sternhartz, p. 149).

Herein lies the problem of the rebbe. He must consciously and deliberately enter the realm of the hasid's pain. It might seem that this repeated exposure to pain would make the rebbe phobic of hasidim and their problems. But phobias come only to those who successfully escape pain and thus reinforce the need to escape. The rebbe, by entering the realm of the pain and fear of the hasid, extinguishes the dread.

Another factor making for the rebbe's repeated exposure to the pain which the hasid brings him is his love for the hasid. The pain and the joy of meeting a beloved, and of interacting with him, have the effect of cancelling one another to some extent. Furthermore, some of the pain and dread are already diminished when the hasid comes to see the rebbe. This is the function of the hasid's empathy. Like a mature patient, who comes to the physician and assumes the physician's clinical detachment to be able to discuss symptoms and prognosis, the hasid comes to the rebbe with his symptoms readied and described in the *quittel* (short note), ready to hear the rebbe's prescription.

In order that the hasid not become confused and bring the rebbe a problem which is not according to his own rung, the *Lyozhna Taqqanoth* (Hielman, 1953, p. 59) demanded that he write his *quittel* at home. The *quittel* thus serves the purpose of bringing the hasid "back to reality." This is especially significant in connection with the hasid's mental image of himself, which may block investment and communication. When the rebbe has the *quittel* before him, he can ensure that the hasid's "real" problem is discussed, rather than the problem which the hasid has come to see as his own under the influence of the environment of the rebbe's court.

The stand which the hasid assumes when facing the rebbe helps the rebbe to keep his psychic distance. He retains his awareness of himself as "rebbe," and the hasid who stands before him expects the rebbe to see him *sub specie aeternitatis*. The rebbe cannot become completely lost in the hasid's pain, since the hasid, by his presence, demands that the rebbe help him in an objective fashion.

Because the hasid comes to the rebbe prepared to change certain conditions of his life, the rebbe must work in the direction of the results he and the hasid envision. This factor serves to change the focus of the interactions from the identification and investment to the objective result, and thus factilitates the psychic distance between rebbe and hasid. At the same time, the rebbe, having attained this psychic distance, cannot prescribe for the hasid's real condition unless he sees it as that of a person in a specific situation. Therefore, he must situate himself in the hasid once more by reinvestment.

It is important to understand that the movement which we are here describing is not that of the rebbe vacillating between two different poles of consciousness. Instead, the rebbe expands his consciousness to encompass both poles. This causes a great tension. Yet, the greater the tension in the rebbe, and the more willingly he maintains it, the more creative will be his insight into the hasid's problem, and the wider will be the scope of his counsel. As Katz explains it:

> Part of our self is fused with the identity of the other. Yet another part of our feeling and thinking is capable of responding to this experience as the external thing it is. (1963, p. 44)

The creative tension which arises from the rebbe's encompassing these two poles enables him to find a fresh approach to *ezah* (counsel).

XI

Even when the rebbe is ready to give the hasid a prescription *(ezah)* for his condition, he must be invested in the hasid in order to see the prescription in terms of the hasid's life situation. The story of R. Michael of Zlotchev bears mentioning. It was he who once gave a harsh penance to a simple Jew who arrived late Friday afternoon from a business trip and barely made it home in time for the Shabbat. It was not until he found himself in a similar situation and the Besht pointed out to him that the contrition of the simple Jew was as great as his own, that R. Michael realized that his penance had been too harsh (Kahane, 1922, p. 66). Thus, the rebbe must himself taste the discipline he prescribes in order to know what it can do for the penitent. This he does by investment.

The rebbe's investment in his hasid at the time of prescription must take into consideration one important factor: the *halakhic* etiquette of seeking the severe ruling for oneself and the lenient one for others. The rebbe who himself would be prepared to work through a severe regimen must not burden his hasid with the same. It is not necessarily a lack of generosity on the part of the hasid if he finds a regimen given by the rebbe too harsh. There may be some very real and worthy commitments which he, in his life situation, cannot ignore, though they may stand in conflict with the rebbe's prescription. The rebbe will therefore grant the hasid's generosity in wishing to follow his counsel, and yet not demand of him the straining of other relationships which in themselves make demands on the hasid's resources.

The rebbe may be aware that his hasid feels an exaggerated guilt over a sin which is not as severe as the hasid feels it to be. Here the rebbe faces a dilemma which he cannot, but by his own empathetic investment, resolve. If he gives the hasid a penance that is in consonance with his guilt feelings, he will be able to help the hasid overcome them. However, in order to help the hasid properly atone for his sins, the rebbe must be able to make him aware of the relative lightness of his transgression. In this way, the burden of guilt can be channeled into areas where it is better employed. The hasid who feels great guilt about a ritual infraction, but is lax on interpersonal ethical levels, needs to be helped to see his guilt where it really exists.

There is another reason why the rebbe will not accept the hasid's harsh estimate of his own guilt. Hopefully, the interaction between rebbe and hasid will achieve in the latter a more mature view of good and evil.

> Truth is a middle path. It wants not to turn to the right by making things more difficult, by finding unreasonable faults and sins in oneself which one has not committed. Nor does it want to turn to the left, to ease one's sense of duty due to self-love in the doing of good works. Both of them, left and right, are false ways. (Schneerson, 1956, p. 32)

When the hasid is able to achieve a more mature view of good and evil, the proportionally true weight of an infraction will become known to him. If the rebbe has weighed his guilt harshly, the hasid will be resentful. He will react by saying: "I did not know how ill or good my acts were. But the rebbe did know, and he let me suffer needlessly." This will shake any real confidence and trust the hasid has in the rebbe, and jeopardize future transactions and growth. The hasid's resentment is bound to result in at least a partial rejection of the rebbe's hierarchy of values. On the other hand, if the rebbe does not help the hasid to atone for his guilt, the hasid will, in all probability, become involved in a greater sin in order to justify a greater penance. Or, he may take out his aggression by projecting his own guilt onto others. In either case, he will have found a way of dealing with his excessive guilt feelings.

The rebbe can help the hasid to deal with his guilt feelings in a positive rather than a negative manner. However, short of complete empathetic investment, the rebbe will fail the hasid in his prescription, and the hasid will be forced to utilize his own resources to deal with his guilt feelings.

By the time the rebbe is ready to prescribe for his hasid at the close of the yehidut, he may have at least partially divested himself in order not to become "lost" in the hasid. If this is the case, he will have to become reinvested in the hasid in order that his *ezah* (counsel) be truly relevant to the hasid's condition. By doing so, he will be able to "see" the effect of his *ezah* on the hasid's life. Only then will he be able to prescribe in the sure knowledge that his prescription is *the* prescription which speaks to the hasid's present life situation, while at the same time taking into account his ongoing life process.

XII

In spite of his natural and hereditary endowment, his gifts of the spirit, and his acquired skill and wisdom, the rebbe still faces the possibility of missing the mark in relating to and empathizing with his hasid. The rebbe is aware that two opposing forces operate within him: 1. logic and reason, coupled with reality testing; and 2. his unconscious *ruach hakodesh* (holy spirit), which is coupled with his intuition and empathy. The faculty of reason tends to thwart the workings of the unconscious processes which are so vital to the rebbe in yehidut.

In addition to being able to effectively analyze the hasid's problem in situation, the rebbe must be able to so liberate his intuitive and empathetic processes that he will be able to freely empathize with his hasid. "The effective empathizer succeeds in getting an inside appreciation of his client" (Katz, 1963, p. 161). However, there is some danger in yielding to unconscious processes. There is almost no recourse to reality testing.

> The participation may have been so engrossing and so irreversible that the practitioner overidentifies with his client and disqualifies himself for the disinterested analysis that is necessary. (Katz, 1963, p. 162)

The Kabbalah and the teachings of Hasidism have taught the rebbe the need to utilize his *hush haziyur* (imaginative faculty). Hayim Vital and the Bratzlaver refer to this faculty as the holy *m'dameh* (imaginative quality). R. Nachman warns that the *m'dameh* of the person whose mind has not yet been cleared of the troubling "yeast" is unreliable. Such a person will tend to project, while assuming that he is actually empathizing.

> What is essential to our understanding of empathy is the idea that it is the experience of another person that we take in rather than an experience of our own which we project onto another. In this phase, we introduce into our own consciousness something that is partly alien and foreign to us. It is another way in which we reduce the social distance between ourselves and others. (Katz, 1963, p. 43)

If the rebbe becomes anxious about entering into the strange and anxiety-producing realm of the hasid's sin, if he cannot conceive of himself as being involved in even the most subtle aspect of that sin, he will be blocked in his investment and will be powerless to help the hasid. It is often possible to descend into a familiar hell, but one that is unfamiliar is more hellish. Or, to quote R. Nachman,

A rebbe must be able to go to any of the twenty-four supernal courts to plead for his hasid. If he does not know the court at which the case is to be tried, or if he does not know the way to the court, he cannot help his hasid. (Sternhartz, p. 141)

The rebbe is the model for the hasidic community and his teaching is the norm of the community. The form of signature which he uses, "the insignificant one," stresses self-derogation; yet he is also authoritarian—he "calls the shots." He is ethnocentric, (Russian vs. Polish, Polish vs. Litvak, Galician vs. Hungarian, etc.), fundamentalist, and stresses conformity to the highly specialized hasidic "ought." All these factors militate against a high degree of empathy. Yet the rebbe needs this empathy, and in order to attain it, he has to draw on his love for all Israel, and for his fellow-man. This love, which extends to the greatest sinner even more abundantly than that of a father to his child, can again lead the rebbe to become overengrossed, and the rebbe must guard against swinging to this pole.

XIII

Because of his capacity for empathy, the rebbe is able to gain knowledge of his hasid which the latter would otherwise not reveal. This fact, and the fact of the rebbe's vertical position vis-a-vis his hasid in the hasidic hierarchy, create yet another difficulty in the rebbe-hasid relationship. If the rebbe uses the knowledge he has gained through empathy in a judgmental manner, it will be to the detriment of his relationship with his hasid. If, however, he is able to overcome this tendency to be judgmental, the mutual empathy between rebbe and hasid will be able to flow more freely. The following hasidic stories illustrate this point.

A respected woman once came to ask the advice of the rabbi of Apt. The instant he set eyes on her he shouted: "Adulteress! You sinned only a short while ago, and yet now you have the insolence to step into this pure house!" Then from the depths of her heart the woman replied: "The Lord of the world has patience with the wicked. He is in no hurry to make them pay their debts and he does not disclose their secret to any creature, lest they be ashamed to turn to him. Nor does he hide his face from them. But the rabbi of Apt sits there in his chair and cannot resist revealing at once what the Creator has covered." From that time on the rabbi of Apt used to say: "No one ever got the better of me except once—and then it was a woman." (Buber, 1948, p. 111)

In a related anecdote,

Rabbi Naftali, a disciple of the rabbi of Apt, who later became the rabbi of Roptchitz, asked a fellow pupil to find out what their teacher thought of him. For half a year his friend made every effort to get the rabbi to say something, but he said nothing about Naftali, nothing good and nothing bad. So his fellow disciple told Naftali, saying: "You see, the master has a golden scale in his mouth. He never passes judgment on anyone, for fear he might wrong him. Has he not forbidden us to judge even those who are supposed wicked through and through? For if anyone were to wrong them, he would be wronging God himself." (Buber, 1948, p. 112)

Both these stories are told of the Apter Rebbe. They illustrate how he had to learn, painfully, not to misuse his empathetic understanding by passing judgment. The beauty of the first story lies in the fact that one of those whom he would judge was the very one to teach him the lesson. The second story illustrates how this lesson became intrinsic to the rebbe's manner of relating to his hasidim.

At times, the rebbe may think that he is invested in his hasid and is fully empathizing with him, when he is not. The rebbe will not generally admit that he has missed the hasid's reality in his investment, and, since implicit belief in the rebbe is part of the hasidic behavior syndrome, the hasid will not admit that the rebbe has missed the mark. If the rebbe has not invested himself properly in the hasid, the hasid will maintain that the rebbe has seen something in him that he is not yet aware of himself. Thus, the rebbe's "miss" becomes a "hit" as a result of a self-fulfilling prophecy; the hasid will live up to the rebbe's expectations of him.

The rebbe may realize that he is unable to invest himself in his hasid as fully as he wishes. At this point, he may, like the Middle Rebbe and the Zemah Zedek, interrupt the yehidut and enter seclusion in order to fast and pray. This, he hopes, will bring him to recover his own repressed material, so that when he becomes aware of it, he will be ready to resume his interview, having discovered the condition of the hasid as it obtains in him on the subtle level. Mending it in himself, he has found a solution that he can recommend to his hasid.

Psychoanalytically considered, the rebbe is anxious that his lack of empathy with a particular hasid may be due to his own repression of evil. He fears that unless he finds the evil within himself, he will not be able to prescribe, since any prescription will necessarily involve a projection of that evil of which he is unconscious.

Hence, a paradox ensues. The rebbe is not properly empathizing with his hasid. When he prescribes, he fails to prescribe for the hasid because he is too busy prescribing for himself; yet he is unaware that he harbors this evil, even in its subtlest form. The paradox is that while unaware of his own condition, he prescribes for it.

The skilled rebbe will avoid such situations. Instead, by placing himself in the presence of God in a penitential manner, and by utilizing fasting and examination of conscience, he will become distracted from his problem. Then by reciting psalms, the rebbe will allow his own problem to confront him as an intrusion into his psalm chanting. It may be that one of the sentences will suddenly take on a new dimension of insight, or the thought will rise as an extraneous thought to disturb him in his chanting. In this sense, the inclination for evil contributes to its own defeat via the rebbe's ruse.

If the rebbe finds that, in spite of all his efforts, he is still unable to empathize with his hasid, he will refer him to another rebbe. R. Levi Yitzchak of Berditchev once interrupted an interview and sent a hasid away. The hasid had been illicitly involved with a woman, and, as the hasid put it, "We waited until she had completed her seven clean days." The hasid then went to R. Shneur Zalman, who was able to help him. The passionate R. Levi Yitzchak could not empathize with one who had been deliberate in his deviation from the law, while at the same time trying to satisfy the law. Had the man sinned in a moment of passion, he could have helped him.

In this case, it was a matter of temperamental incompatibility which upset the rebbe's empathy. If the hasid had not waited the seven clean days and had sinned in passion, R. Levi Yitzchak could have helped him by prescribing an equally passionate surrender to God and his purposes. This he actually did on another occasion when he met a man on the street who had a reputation all over Berditchev for his amorous pursuits. R. Levi Yitzchak said to him: "I envy you. You have so many acts of love on your conscience. If only you would turn to God with your passionate love, he would turn all your sins into merit, and you would be greater in His eyes than many a saint."

In spite of his natural gifts, and his awareness of his own mission, the pitfalls which the rebbe faces are many, and the fact of the great depths and the many levels which his vision opens to him means that the pitfalls are even deeper. The rebbe must have the capacity to maintain a delicate balance between the two poles of the investment continuum. He must rid himself of all factors and attitudes which would inhibit free empathy and investment, while at the same time guarding carefully against becoming overengrossed in his hasid.

XIV

As an effective empathizer, the rebbe can trust himself and his reactions. As rebbe, he need not be defensive. He can enjoy his inner secu-

rity precisely because he knows where, on the subtle level, he himself
is vulnerable. This enables him to identify freely. When the rebbe
sighs, he shares his hasid's anxieties. This he does freely and without
fear of contagion. His self-scrutiny keeps him from falling into the
traps laid by his own needs. He manages his counter-transference
without allowing it to beguile him (Katz, 1963, p. 146). Therefore,
rebbe and hasid can speak freely of their love for one another. Each has
a strong emotional investment in the other. So ideal is this love that,
according to a popular hasidic saying, had King Solomon known of
rebbe and hasid, he would have written the Canticle about them instead.

While the love between rebbe and hasid rarely assumes any of the
manifest forms which are normally associated with an expression of
love, there are a great many stylized gestures which express this love.
When the rebbe teaches, he "inseminates" the hasid, who then gives
birth to the rebbe's seed in the form of Torah and mitzvot (good deeds).
In the hasidic system of correspondences, to teach someone who does
not absorb the teaching, or who is unworthy, is likened to masturba-
tion and results in a nocturnal emission on the part of the rebbe.

The rebbe who feels such love for a hasid that he is moved to kiss
him, will sublimate this feeling and instead give him a special teaching discourse. Sometimes the rebbe will show his love by sharing his
food and wine.

The love between rebbe and hasid can at times be very fierce and
jealous. This accounts for the great concern that is aroused when a
hasid leaves one rebbe for another. To do so arouses the rebbe's
qpaydah (wrathful contempt). The rebbe feels that the hasid has in a
sense spurned him and has demeaned the love that was between them.

The rebbe's love for his hasid does not blind him to the hasid's
realities. He does not permit his vision of the hasid to become clouded
by his love for him. He is trained to love the hasid in "the manner of
Abraham," a love that is governed by reason and by a commitment to
God, and not with "the love of Ishmael," in which the reason behind the
love is obscured. In other words, Abraham loves in order to bring souls
to God. Ishmael loves because he loves, and he possesses in his love.

For the rebbe, the criterion by which he judges his love for his hasid
is the extent to which he is content to leave the hasid in the hands of
Divine providence. By so doing, the rebbe should have no difficulty
disengaging his attention and emotions from the hasid. He is to look at
each soul in the way in which it stands in the primal thought of *Adam
Kadmon* (man in God's conception). The rebbe sacrifices the hasid for
the sanctification of God's name. This process is somewhat akin to the

process in which R. Elimelekh counsels his hasid to cast himself, in his imagination, into a fierce fire for the sake of God. In *hitpashtut*—divestment—the rebbe can drown the hasid in "grace" or in "fire" (Elimelekh of Lizensk, 1956).

By surrendering the hasid to the fire, the rebbe frees both himself and the hasid from the attachment. The proper perspective is then re-established, and both rebbe and hasid belong once more to God and not to each other. The manipulative and possessive aspects of their love are removed, so that rebbe and hasid are realigned to face God instead of each other. In this posture, the rebbe regains a greater degree of objectivity.

Although it is vital to the yehidut that rebbe and hasid empathize with one another, it is equally vital that neither assume the role of the other. The rebbe must not do what the hasid should do for himself, and the hasid must not presume to do the rebbe's task. It is as destructive to try to raise a hasid beyond his level as it is not to help him at all. Under these circumstances, the progress of the hasid will, at best, be of very short duration, and his fall may cause him great harm.

By divesting himself from the hasid, the rebbe is able to distinguish what the hasid, "according to his own rung," must do, so that his prescription will be one that speaks to the hasid's condition.

There is almost no material discussing the possibility of the rebbe's hangover from hasid to hasid. One must, however, assume that the same process discussed under investment applies also to divestment, since any succeeding investment is blocked by an incomplete divestment from the preceding hasid.

If, in confronting one hasid, the rebbe notices a confusion of persons before him, he will be aware that he is still speaking to the previous hasid rather than to the one who now stands before him. If he can negotiate an immediate switch back to the hasid who confronts him, he will do so. If not, he will, as in the case of blocked investment, terminate the interview and work through his involvement. The best method of overcoming the block is to "recite a chapter of the Psalms" for the hasid with whom he is still involved, and then leave him in God's hands. If the divestment is still not achieved, the rebbe may turn to more introspective methods, and perhaps seek solitude and penance. If he is still not ready to resume the interview, he can summon the presence of special persons, who, by being available to hear other things from the rebbe, can divert him and free him from his blocked divestment. Or, he may call such persons in order to tell them an analogous *ma'asseh* (story), which gives him the possibility of working things out.

Only when the rebbe has fully divested himself from one hasid is he
ready to empathize with and invest in the next hasid. When he finds
his divestment blocked, he must utilize every means at his disposal in
order to free himself from the block so that he can once more be at the
service of his hasid and of God.

References

Agnon, S.J. *Lifnim min hahomah*. Jerusalem: Schocken Books, 1975.
Berger, I. *Sepher zechut yisroel*. Jerusalem: Jerusalem Hebrew Book Store, 1954. (Originally published, 1906.)
Buber, M. *Tales of the hasidim* (2 vols.) New York: Schocken Books, 1948.
Elimelekh of Lizensk (18th Century). *Sepher noam Elimelekh*. New York: Israel Ze'ev, 1956.
Frankl, V. E. *Psychotherapy and existentialism: Selected papers on logotherapy*. New York: Simon and Schuster, 1968.
Hayman, A. *Ozar divray hahakhamiym upithgameyhem*. Tel Aviv: "Dvir" Publication Society, 1955.
Heilman, D.Z. (Ed.) *Igrot baal hatanya ubney doro*. Jerusalem: Mesorah Publishing Co., 1953.
The Holy Scriptures (2 vols.) Philadelphia: Jewish Publication Society, 1917.
Kahane, A. *Sefer hahasidut*. Warsaw: Die Welt Publications, 1922.
Katz, R.L. *Empathy: Its nature and uses*. London: Collier-Macmillan Ltd., 1963.
Kleinman, M.D. (Ed.) *Or yesharim*. Jerusalem: Private publication by anonymous Slonimer Hasid, 1958.
Klopholtz, I. (Ed.) *Sepher hahassiydut mitorat belz* (2 vols) Jerusalem: Belzer Institute, 1965.
Maimonides, M. (12th Century). *Commentary on the mishnah* (J. Kapach, translator). Jerusalem: Mossad Harav Kook, 1967.
The Midrash (10 vols.) H. Friedman & M. Simon (Eds.) London: Soncino Press, 1961.
Mordecai of Lekhovitz (18th Century) et al. *Torat avot*. Jerusalem: Yeshivat Bet Avrohom of Jerusalem, 1961.
Nachman of Bratzlav (18th Century) in Nathan of Nemirov (Ed.) *Meshivath. Nephesh*. Jerusalem: Hasidei Bratzlav, 1960.
Schneerson, J.I. Hayom yom. Brooklyn: Kehot Publication Society, 1956.
Schneerson, J.I. *Kuntres hay elul*. Brooklyn: Kehot Publication Society, 1955.
Schneerson, J.I. *Sefer hamaamorim—Kuntreism*. Warsaw: Kadimah Press, 1935.
Schneerson, M. (Ed.) *Sefer toldot Maharash*. Brooklyn: Ozar Hachasidim—Lubavitch, 1947.
Schneerson, S.D.B. *Kuntres umayon mibeyt haShem*. Brooklyn: Kehot Publication Society, 1958.
Schneerson, S.D.B. *Torat shalom: Sepher hasiyot*. Brooklyn: Ozar Hahasidim Lubavitch, 1946.
Schneur Zalman of Liadi (18th Century). *Liqqutei amarim: Tanya* (Vol. 1) (N. Mindel, trans.) Brooklyn: Kehot Publication Society, 1965. (a)
Schneur Zalman of Liadi (18th Century). *Liqqutei amarim: Tanya* (Vol. 2) (N. Mangel, trans.) Brooklyn: Kehot Publication Society, 1965. (b)
Shapira, K. *Esh kodesh*. Tel Aviv: Va'ad Chasidei Piasetzno, 1960.
Sternhartz, N. *Shivehay Haran*. Jerusalem: Hevrat Hasidey Bratzlav, no date.
The Talmud (18 Vols.) I. Epstein (Ed.) London: Soncino Press, 1961.
Ze'ev Volf of Zhitomir (18th Century). *Sepher or hameir*. New York: Ziv Publishing Company, 1954.

The Kabbalah, Hasidism, and the Life of Unification

Jonathan S. Woocher

This paper is a case study in the meeting of psychology and religion, not as modern categories and disciplines, but as dimensions of the life and thought of the Jewish people, and specifically of two movements—the Kabbalah and Hasidism. These two great expressions of the mystical strand in Judaism developed out of the needs and hopes of the Jews of the Middle Ages, Jews exiled from their homeland, dispersed among often hostile peoples with faiths purporting to supercede Judaism, and repeatedly facing the spiritual dangers of despair and internal disintegration alongside the physical threats emanating from their neighbors.

Against this background, the Kabbalah, and later Hasidism, emerged as major forces in Jewish life. The Kabbalah was an elaborate mystical, mythological, and practical system which transmuted and transvalued Jewish religious ideas and ritual, making them serve a grand vision of historical and spiritual redemption. Hasidism, developing in Eastern Europe in the 18th century, absorbed the teachings of the Kabbalah and combined them with spontaneous religious fervor to create an unparalleled communal mysticism and ethos.

The Kabbalah and Hasidism dealt directly with what today would be called the "psychological" dimension of human existence in their prescriptions for a Jewish pattern of life which could overcome the agonies and anxieties of mundane historical and social experience. They did so, however, in an overtly religious context and language, as part of an encounter with the Ultimate which served as the basis both for a struggle against evil and suffering in the world and for a quest for personal wholeness and fulfillment.

It would be impossible to describe here either the totality or the "essence" of Jewish mystical teaching and all of its elaborate cosmological, theosophical, ethical, and ritual expressions in their actual historical context. Instead, drawing on the work of some of Jewish mysticism's greatest modern interpreters, this paper will briefly examine four key dimensions of its life and thought: the mystical symbolization of existence as "exile" and estrangement; its vision and prescription of a path to restoration and reunification; the image of fulfilled human existence embodied in hasidic teaching; and the hasidic understanding of the "therapeutic" roles of genuine leadership and community. The question of how from these dimensions of Jewish mysticism one may be able to derive insights which can be incorporated into the contemporary meeting of psychology and religion will then be explored.

II

For the kabbalist and the hasid, the primary reality of mundane existence was the fact of exile—exile physically from one's historical homeland and exile spiritually from the intimate communion with God to which one aspired. "Exile" served for the Jewish mystics as a profound symbol which could focus not only on their own historical and religious experience, but on the very condition of the cosmos itself as one of existential estrangement. Beyond even the national exile of the Jewish people and the exile of the human soul from its Divine Root, the Kabbalah and Hasidism envisaged an exile of all of the "holy sparks" of the Divine creative light, now scattered throughout creation as a result of a vast cosmic accident and trapped in "shells" which prevent their reunification with their source. Even more boldly, the Jewish mystics spoke of part of God himself—the Shekhina, or Indwelling Presence—as in exile with the Jewish people, in need of reunion with God alongside each human soul (Scholem, 1961; 1965; Buber, 1960).

In this symbolization of the human and cosmic condition, Jewish mysticism found a far-reaching key to understanding all of the problematics of human existence. Exile, at its roots, is separation, the disruption or sundering of what is meant to be unified or harmoniously

related. In this light, evil can be seen as another species of exilic separation. As both an ethical and a metaphysical reality, evil is that
which severs or restrains, that which prevents the consummation of
integration and relationship; or, conversely, it is that which forces
elements into relationships for which they were not intended. Human
sin either destroys a union or creates an illicit one. On the deepest
metaphysical level, the existence of evil is seen by Jewish mysticism as
an expression of the Divine self-estrangement. It results from the isolation of God's quality of "strict judgment" from its ideally correspond-
ing quality of Divine "mercy" (Krakovsky, 1950; Scholem, 1961).

Nowhere is both the immediacy and the depth of the kabbalist and
hasidic understanding of existence as "exile" more graphically illustrated than in the mystical development of the symbol of God's self-
estrangement—the exile of the Shekhina. In kabbalist theosophy the
Shekhina is the tenth and last of God's creative potencies (*sefirot*), but
even more, the Shekhina is the feminine aspect of divinity, the Wife,
Mother, or Daughter who must be united with her masculine counterpart among the *sefirot*—the generative, active power of God—if all of
God's powers are to be harmoniously united and the world sustained by
Divine compassion.

This identification of a feminine dimension of the Deity, more, the
symbolization of God's unity in a sublime harmony of masculine and
feminine principles, constituted a radical break with normative Jewish
thought. But it enabled the kabbalists to link their vision of cosmic
exile and restoration to the primal human experiences of sexual differentiation, desire, and union. The separation of the Shekhina from
her consort epitomizes and underlies the "exilic" character of human
existence. With even God in exile, it can be no wonder that the world is
experienced as one of painful separations—between good and evil,
judgment and mercy, male and female, rich and poor, desire and
conscience—which subject humanity to a host of "demonic" powers,
both within and surrounding each individual. One cannot help but
reflect in one's own soul and conduct the divisions within God. Indeed,
the human being is a dynamic contradiction, a creature in and of a
world filled with disunities, who aspires, nevertheless, to realize the
self as the image of a unified God the self was meant to be. In the
seamless continuity of the mystical cosmos, the person, in seeking to
end personal exile, intuits that only when the exile of all being—
including God's—is overcome will one's own be concluded as well
(Scholem, 1965).

The Jewish mystical theology of exile can thus be seen as a bold
assertion that the problematics of human experience—the phenomena

called alienation, anxiety, estrangement, and conflict—are all, in truth, manifestations of a single deep rent in the fabric of being. For the Kabbalah and Hasidism, the condition of exile was one shared by all, one which transcended the categories of inner personal experience and social historical life, and one which could be brought to an end only when all domains of existence and all creatures, as bearers of the exiled "holy sparks," were redeemed from the power of separation and disharmony.

III

In this light, the challenge facing Jewish mysticism was to point the way towards unification, towards the overcoming of psychic, social, and spiritual exile. Although the unity underlying this disoriented world might always be perceived by a mystic elite, the Kabbalah taught that the realization of this unity in fact depends upon human activity as well as human vision. Precisely as a two-fold being—a bridge between God and the world—one's task is to lift the world to God in and through one's own person. Thus, the highest religious value for the Kabbalah of the Zohar, the mystical classic, was *devekut,* a continuous loving attachment or adhesion to God.

The establishment of this direct relationship to God, though certainly a contemplative process, was nevertheless not predicated on special modes of consciousness or detachment from the life of the community. *Devekut* was a social-ethical as well as personal religious value; other individual and communal virtues—charity, prayer, penitence—were regarded by the mystics as means toward its realization (Scholem, 1961).

As might be expected, the epitome of the work of unification for the early kabbalists was to be found in the task of "reuniting God and God's Shekhina." The redemption of humankind from exile and sin can only be achieved when the masculine and feminine aspects of Divinity are once again joined in harmonious union and the flow of God's compassionate grace through the world is once more unimpeded (Krakovsky, 1950).

Effecting the reunion of God and the Shekhina thus became the constant aim of kabbalist prayer, ritual, and action. The foremost mundane reflection of this desired heavenly "marriage" of God's active and passive, procreating and conceiving potencies was, quite logically, the sexual union of man and woman in earthly marriage. Thus, for Jewish mysticism, the love between husband and wife became a redemptive force (Scholem, 1965). But even more, no wholeness and completion is possible for the individual unless the individual is, in the words of the Zohar (1963, p. 34), "male and female." In Jewish mystical exegesis and in other Jewish sources (Talmud, *Berakhot,* 61a), Adam was originally created androgynous, and after the division into male and female took place, "only when Eve was made perfect, was he then made perfect too" (Zohar, quoted in Scholem, 1949/1963, p. 33). Thus, just as the condition of exile was bound up with masculine/feminine separation, so too for the kabbalists was redemption linked to the achievement of sexual harmony and integration.

The 16th century kabbalist system of Rabbi Isaac Luria elaborated on the earlier assertion of one's potential for effecting the reunion of God and the Shekhina into a full-fledged program of *tikkun* (restoration or correction). According to the Lurianic myth, it is one's purpose as the crown of all created being to initiate the reordering of all that had been disordered in the great cosmic catastrophe at the beginning of time. One must not only reunite the Divine "family" by restoring the Shekhina to her consort; one must as well begin to gather up all the "holy sparks" of the Great Soul of all humankind and purge the world of the demonic power of the "shells" in which they have been trapped.

This work of *tikkun,* Luria taught, was accomplished not only through prayer, ritual, and mystical meditations, but also through observance of any of the commandments of the Torah, which was seen as the mystical Law of the *tikkun.* Just as each sin plunges one's soul and the Shekhina deeper into exile, so too each pious or virtuous act brings souls closer to their Divine Root. Evil is both pushed back and robbed of its active power as the sparks are liberated and God's justice and mercy reunited, leaving the shells as an ineffectual residue (Scholem, 1965). The completion of the process of *tikkun* would mean the complete restoration of cosmic and spiritual harmony, the true fulfillment of God's plan of creation. In this way, the unification which the Jew can and must help to effect constituted for the Lurianic kabbalists the true eschatological event, to be marked at its completion by Israel's Messianic restoration (Scholem 1961; 1965).

IV

Lurianic Kabbalah nourished the Messianic yearnings of the Jewish masses, but the tragedy of the 17th century, which saw both violent persecutions and a false mystical Messiah, demanded a recasting of the program of unification. Hasidism, under the leadership of Israel Baal Shem Tov, provided this new program by de-emphasizing Messianic activism and focusing its teaching on the redemption of the individual soul and the gathering up of the "holy sparks" scattered throughout creation. In this reconstruction of the link between personal and cosmic unification, the reunion of God and the Shekhina retained its central symbolic role, but was tied more intimately to the individual's effort to bring the whole physical/spiritual being into a unity of intention and action (Scholem, 1961).

This unity of personal being—this *yichud* or *kavannah* (intent), above and beyond the Lurianic *yichudim* and *kavannot* (intents), the mystical meditations attached to particular deeds—became in hasidic teaching the unifying force for the cosmos as a whole. Hasidism thereby offered a redemptive program which was directed less towards an immediate eschatological conclusion than towards a transformation of everyday reality into the substance of spiritual unification (Buber, 1960).

In its image of fulfilled existence, Hasidism envisioned a life embodying psychological wholeness, interhuman community, and intimacy with the Absolute. The goal of the hasid, as for the Kabbalist, was a life of *devekut* and *hitlahavut* (ecstasy), a life in which one is joyfully bound up in the actual life of God, an unfolding of the soul which flows into the Absolute. But as was true for the earlier kabbalists, hasidic *hitlahavut* did not demand physical retreat from the world; indeed, just the opposite, for the life of ecstasy was also the life of service (*avodah*).

For Hasidism, service meant unification, the transformation of that concrete portion of time and space allotted to each person into a more unified, more harmonious reality. Hasidism taught that one can serve in whatever one does—in prayer, work, recreation, family life—through *kavannah,* the directing of all of one's thoughts and actions toward the Divine Unity. Both in one's "receiving" and one's "giving"—i.e., in the utilization of what is provided in life and in the creative expression and realization of one's own potentials—*kavannah* can help to liberate "holy sparks" for reunification with God. *Kavannah, avodah,* and *hitlahavut* all flow together and are consummated in the life of the individual of *shiflut,* humility or simplicity.

In hasidic teaching, humility did not mean self-abnegation. Rather, it was the paradoxical recognition of both one's unique task and one's essential identity with all people. The humble, or simple person became an ideal for Hasidism as the person who can live directly with others, who does the entrusted good with a unified strength. Such a person does not pretend to know what is beyond personal capacities until at least attempting what must be done; and sometimes, through a response of grace, the humble person discovers previously unknown resources in the self. Such a person performs the highest service of all:

loving and helping one's fellow being, and thereby realizing concretely the unity of all souls, with each other and God (Buber, 1958).

Hasidism taught that the transformation of the world and its unification with God are intimately bound up with one's ability to unify one's own being. Each individual must search one's heart, try to discover the particular way in which one is called to serve, and resolve the self, body and soul, into a unified existence. Conflicts between people can only be resolved when each individual resolves the conflict within the self and unifies thought, speech, and action. Self-unification is not, however, the end: one must turn to the world and its redemption, and make this the aim of one's action. In hasidic terminology, the unification of the "lower" and "upper" worlds only takes place through holy life in *this* world, through exposing the place where one stands to God's presence and lifting it to God (Buber, 1958).

Even evil, dependent as it is upon Divine energy for its force, can be brought into this process of unification, since it is really in need only of direction in order to become good. The temptations which bedevil the person, the urges to sin and demonic fantasies, are clothed in evil, but the force of desire comes from God and needs simply to be redirected towards the person for its unifying potential to be realized.

According to this hasidic conception, imagination and sensuality— "alien thoughts" and the "evil inclination"—are not the person's enemies, simply to be repressed, but the raw substance of what can become positive action if they are given direction. The inner conflicts which trouble the human psyche are meant to be taken up in a higher integration in which the full energy of the psyche is used to build a loving relationship between people, and between people and God. Even the act of sinning is not irreparable, for in the sin itself the Divine force is still present, ready to be released as *t'shuvah,* the "turning" back to God (Buber, 1958; 1960). In the face of human failing, what must be avoided above all is despair, because *it* makes the turning impossible (Buber, 1947/1961, p. 315).

Perhaps no activity better epitomizes the hasidic quest for unification than does their prayer. In directing the creative power of the word to God, prayer constituted for Hasidism one's supreme effort to unify one's own soul, to unite it with the souls of one's fellow beings, and to raise all of these souls to God. Prayer is therapeutic in the deepest sense; it transports the individual to a higher level of unification in his existence. But it is also an awesome venture; one risks one's very being in throwing oneself into prayer, in opening oneself completely to God. Only then can one possibly experience the ecstasy of unification.

Alongside prayer, the hasidim saw in song and dance paths to and expressions of the spontaneous joy of a unified existence. Sometimes, where even words cannot go or transport the person, pure melody and rhythm, transcending the conscious and the unconscious, can. Whether wild and joyous or tender and sad, the hasidic song and dance can help one to infuse one's entire being with and unite a whole community around an utterance of one's deepest sensibility (Jacobs, 1973; Minkin, 1935/1971; Rabinowicz, 1970). The ideal hasidic life is thus one which is open to the full depth of inner and worldly experience, but which is at the same time committed to the responsible direction of every impulse and deed to the service of one's fellow beings and God.

V

The realism of Hasidism's great teachers enabled them to recognize that the achievement of the ideal of joyous service and communion with God was a difficult task for people caught up in the chaos, the pressures, and the delusions of life; for people buffeted by all the forces which assault the unity of the soul. Hasidism provided, however, a helper for the common folk in the person of the zaddik, the leader and heart of the hasidic community. The ideal zaddik served as a healer for the whole person, for the soul and the body. He concentrated not on esoteric learning, but on the substance of everyday life—its griefs, despairs and cares, and its joys. His goal was to help each hasid walk independently toward God, to aid all in realizing the ecstasy and unification that had been achieved (Buber, 1947/1961; Dresner, 1960/1974).

Not all hasidic leaders, to be sure, lived up to this high ideal; some became demi-gods, objects of worship, or mere wonder workers. There were in addition elements of hasidic thought which sought in fact to establish an almost unbridgeable chasm between the zaddik and the ordinary fellow. Yet a number of zaddikim apparently did approach the ideal, and their lives and work constitute graphic illustrations of what the life of unification and the process of genuine "healing" can be. The power of the zaddik lay less in his teaching than in his being. In the imagery of a hasidic tale, the zaddik *is* a Torah—a living revelation of Divine teaching.

To those who came to him for help, the zaddik is a penetrating and concerned mirror, understanding their deepest needs and desires even when these are unspoken. He heals through what Martin Buber (1960) called the "psycho-synthetic" method, confronting the other's divided soul with his own unified being and pulling the other's soul with him until it too becomes whole and can once again protect the unity and health of the body. At times the zaddik must share in the anguish and suffering of those around him, and must even risk becoming entrapped in their sin and despair in order to lift them up. But this risk is essential to his work; a zaddik is no zaddik if he remains an isolated holy man, cut off from those who need his spiritual strength to recover their own (Dresner, 1960/1974).

The relationship of the zaddik and his hasidim is the key to the success of the ongoing therapeutic venture. He unites with the community as its center, kindling a flame within it and being illuminated in turn by that light. He serves as the living bridge between heaven and earth, in intimate communion with God, yet working in the world to infuse it with Divine light and thereby elevating it to the supramundane. He restores to the earth those who become preoccupied with the rarified and lose contact with life, and he raises to heavenly heights those burdened with the weight of the earth. The zaddik is a true union of spirit and nature, and by binding body with soul, person with person, and earth with heaven, his life becomes a *yichud,* a work of unification (Buber, 1960; 1947/1961; Dresner, 1960/1974).

The task of the hasidim is to strive to emulate their zaddik's powerful love in a life of charity, justice, and peace as well as prayer, song, and ecstasy. In absorbing the spiritual strength of the zaddik, the community too achieves an inner harmony. It becomes a fit setting for the reunion of people's souls and the Shekhina itself with God. In such a community the ultimate ideal of the hasidic ethos—an unreserved love between individuals, expressing each person's uniqueness and all peoples' oneness with God—can take root in human life and transform it (Buber, 1958). Even the death of its zaddik can dim life's joy only temporarily for the ideal community, for his death and potentially that of each person can be seen as an affirmation of that life, as a necessary step on the soul's destined journey back to God (Minkin, 1935/1971).

The zaddik and his hasidim constitute a "therapeutic" community by combining concern for each individual, mutual support, serving and teaching leadership, and a guiding vision of universal redemptive possibilities. The hasidic communal ideal rested on a faith in the power of simplicity, joy, and the encounter with a counselor and healer who himself embodied wholeness and intimacy with people and God, to effect a unification embracing all the dimensions of human life. In this ideal, the Jewish mystical quest for unification—for redemption from the many "exiles" which plague the person—reached perhaps its fullest realization. The mystical/Messianic dream became a daily work in which each new step towards psychological, social, and spiritual unification provided a taste of the ultimate unity.

VI

In the discussion of these four central dimensions of kabbalistic and hasidic life and teaching, an attempt has been made to show how these historical movements incorporated significant "psychological"— or perhaps "psychosocial"—components within their mythico-religious worldview and ethos. The Kabbalah and Hasidism were ambitious attempts to mend the ruptured fabric of Jewish existence in its totality, to promote inner wholeness, social brotherhood, and the realization of a cosmic and spiritual harmony which places people in intimate relationship with God and all being.

In order to appreciate this achievement, it may be useful to translate what is taken to be the essential psychosocial teaching of Jewish mysticism into a set of propositions expressed in a contemporary idiom. The Kabbalah and Hasidism teach that

1. The person's fundamental problem is separation, estrangement, and alienation.
2. This estrangement is inherently multi-dimensional; it is internal—reflected in psychic disturbances; social—reflected in conflict and suffering; and spiritual—reflected in a sense of existential homelessness, emptiness, and anxiety. All these aspects are inter-related.
3. What is recognized as "evil" is the result of, or the impulse toward, separation and isolation—the disruption of what should be harmoniously related, the withdrawal of isolated elements from their context in a greater whole, or the improper but willful combination of things which should remain in their proper places.
4. A crucial sign of the estrangement which characterizes existence is the separation of qualities such as "compassion" and "strength," "masculine" and "feminine," into opposing and mutually exclusive principles, rather than complementary qualities which should exist bound up with one another.
5. Human fulfillment depends on the overcoming of separations and the rectification of disharmonious relationships on every level of experience.
6. Within the individual, this work of unification involves resolute efforts to unify one's personality, one's thought, speech, and action. Fantasies and destructive impulses which may cause psychic conflicts can be transformed and integrated into this personal wholeness when their energy is directed towards establishing a responsible "serving" relationship with the world.

7. Between people, unification involves the attempt to resolve conflicts and build community on the basis of the ideal of unreserved love, with respect for each individual's uniqueness and awareness of the unity of all people.

8. Every individual should be regarded as potentially and essentially good, since no one is ultimately entirely evil, as each has a "holy spark." Rather than inducing the person to despair at "sinfulness," the spark of goodness within the person should be encouraged, so that one might "turn" from evil in fact.

9. *Every* act and word can be unifying if performed with one's whole being—body and soul, and with a single-minded intent to further the ultimate unification of all being.

10. An ideal life is one which embodies spontaneity, simplicity, directness in relationship, and joy, as well as responsible service.

11. Each individual has a unique potential and can work for unification in one's own way and from one's own place.

12. Overcoming the separation between male and female or the masculine and feminine is essential to the work of unification and the attainment of personal wholeness. It should be noted, however, that Jewish mysticism did not in practice break essentially with traditional Jewish patterns of male-centeredness and dominance.

13. The conflicts, anxiety, doubts, and suffering of earthly life belong to creation and set the personal task in life; they are neither illusory nor final, and can be surmounted through a life of unification.

14. One never knows what one's full resources are until one attempts the deed asked. Only then does one discover the limits of one's capacities.

15. Activities like prayer, song, and dance, in which one opens the self to one's self and to the world directly and whole-heartedly are especially powerful means to and expressions of unification.

16. Despair is the greatest evil.

17. One individual can help strengthen and support another's effort to unify one's being by seeking to embody unification in one's own life and action.

18. In the healing relationship, one must not try to take over the other's task, but should try to help others recognize their own work and utilize their own potential in its performance.

19. The healing action must be directed from one whole person to the wholeness of the other's being, body and soul; if the "healer" is truly attentive to the person who comes for help, then the healer too can draw strength from the relationship.

20. A loving, mutually supportive community can assist each of its members in the quest for personal wholeness and fulfillment.
21. Even death itself should not be viewed as a negation of life, but seen rather as part of the total redemptive process which affirms life.

VII

These assertions provide a clear framework for confronting problems of human identity, health, and fulfillment. They incorporate both a personality theory and a therapeutic program. In fact, there is far more in Jewish mystical teaching in this regard than has been presented here. Kabbalistic and hasidic teaching do not idealize human experience, but neither do they reduce human life to a meaningless, deterministic process.

Though each of the assertions made in the name of the Jewish mystics ought, of course, to be subject to thorough and objective analysis, none is absurd on its face and each deserves consideration as a contribution to our own understanding of psychosocial reality. Many of these propositions would be endorsed by contemporary psychological theorists, and this raises the question of why one should attend to them at all in their traditional, mythically and theologically laden formulations.

Before attempting to respond to this question, it might be proper to reverse the issue. Why bother reformulating kabbalistic and hasidic teaching at all? To a kabbalist and/or hasid, this presentation of their teaching would almost certainly be unacceptable, if not even unrecognizable, as expressions of their belief and practice. The offering of these formulations is *not* meant to imply that the teachings of the Kabbalah and Hasidism can or should ultimately be removed from their organic context in a Jewish life and community of faith. There can be no genuine meeting between modern psychology and religious traditions if the latter are denuded of their specifically "religious" content in order to be assimilated to the former. On the other hand, attempts at language translation can be important as a means of establishing, precisely, that a common framework of concerns *does* exist, and that religious world-views and life-patterns like those of the Jewish mystics almost always incorporate a substantial "humanistic" dimension within their teaching.

Once this common agenda of concerns is recognized, it becomes possible to bring the Kabbalah and Hasidism into direct dialogue with important movements in modern psychology—Neo-Freudianism, Jungianism, "humanistic" psychologies, Gestalt, even behaviorism—and in philosophy—atheistic and religious existentialisms, Eastern mysticisms, naturalist and process theologies, Marxism—all of which also purport to help people achieve a more harmonious, de-alienated existence.

The Kabbalah and Hasidism are not, to be sure, "scientific" psychologies; nor are they fully developed social theories. Nevertheless, they do make "empirical" statements about the nature of people and of reality, including Ultimate Reality, and they do prescribe a pattern of human conduct which is designed to respond to the problematics of human existence. What is more, both the "empirical" and the "normative" dimensions of Jewish mystical teaching do not represent the conclusions of a single psychologist, therapist, philosopher, or theologian. The claims and norms of the Kabbalah and Hasidism have been the substance of a way of life shared by a significant portion of an entire people. For this reason alone, they deserve serious consideration.

The Kabbalah and Hasidism ought not even here, however, be reduced to historical "laboratories" for testing propositions now better articulated in contemporary, "de-mythologized" terms. To make the meeting between these movements and modern psychology a genuine encounter, one must go one step further: one must confront directly the religious vocabulary and character of their teaching.

The historical power of the Kabbalah and Hasidism for the Jewish people lay largely in their ability to integrate all the dimensions of human experience into a single symbolically-crystallized framework. The religious/mythic dimension of Jewish mysticism energized and provided the keystone for this structure of life and thought. The very vocabulary which modern humanistic thinkers would probably find most problematic—talk of "God and the Shekhina," of "the soul and its Root," of "holy sparks," of "cleaving to the Divine," of "cosmic restoration"—is precisely that which gives this mystical religious life its organic unity, its impelling vision, and its assurance of direction and efficacy.

VIII

The existential psychotherapist Viktor Frankl (1963) has argued that the psychodynamics of human existence are always accompanied by a "noodynamics," a quest on the part of each individual for *meaning*. Religion, as a human phenomenon, centers around this quest to place one's existence in the framework of not only an ordered cosmos, but a humanly meaningful one as well, i.e., a cosmos in which *purpose* in addition to *structure* may be found. Purpose, in turn, implies direction which transcends the personal self and which one is given to fulfill.

From this perspective, the work of psychology and philosophy is not complete if people fail or refuse to come to grips with the problem of direction in human life today. To speak, as many currently popular psychologies do, of "fulfilling one's potentials," "taking charge of one's own life," "self-actualizing," "becoming a person," or "achieving self-integration" is good, as far as it goes. It has herein been suggested that in psychological terms the Kabbalah and Hasidism themselves embody both a "growth-" and a "wholeness-oriented" approach to human personality and social dynamics. Their teaching has clear points of contact with the humanistic psychologies of Carl Rogers, Erich Fromm, Abraham Maslow, and Viktor Frankl, as well as with some analytic approaches.

As living religious movements, however, the Kabbalah and Hasidism transcended their own psychology. By locating the person within the cosmos as a whole, by defining a role for the person in the transformation of all reality, and by providing the individual with a trans-subjective model for the performance of that role through their interpretations of Torah, the Kabbalah and Hasidism linked the psychological, social and noological spheres of human existence to an ultimately meaningful vision of the destiny and purpose of creation.

As a result, the Jewish mystical understanding of human fulfillment did not end with the unification of one's fundamental drives or personality. Neither did it stop with an assertion of the bond between the quest for personal wholeness and the effort to create a community of fellowship and love. The Kabbalah and Hasidism dared to go further, to tie both of these processes to a hidden process—the unification of all being with its Transcendent Source.

It was this final process, expressible only in terms of myth, mystery, and religious symbolism, but capable of being participated in within this world, which established the ultimate meaningfulness of and direction for the psychological and social quest. For the Jewish mystics, this direction was embodied in Torah—the divinely revealed blueprint of creation which prescribes the pathway toward redemption.

The kabbalists and hasidim were not literalists in their understanding of what it meant to fulfill the Torah's commandments; they did not limit redemptive action to the specific injunctions of the tradition. But they were able to look beyond themselves to a reliable guide for the life of unification, one which possessed transcendent authority even as it was actualized in the light of personally experienced mystery.

In the meeting between Jewish mysticism and modern psychology, one encounters again the question of whether any analytic and prescriptive structure grounded solely in a humanistic world-view can fill the place in human life which religious traditions and teachings claim to occupy. The integrating power of myth and the directing force of Torah enabled the Jewish mystic engaged in a quest for personal wholeness and social harmony to see individual efforts as supported and guided by the Power which will ultimately unify all being.

In the context of the process of *tikkun,* the individual's ventures toward unification, however apparently ineffectual, took on a measure of cosmic import. The knowledge that the fate of God depends in part on human thoughts and deeds was undoubtedly awesome and sobering, but it was also a guarantor of human significance. With God's instruction awaiting one's unravelling and implementation, the struggle for *tikkun* and *yichud* was not a desperate leap into the unknown, but passage along a pathway laid out since creation.

The modern being is, if not openly hostile to, at least justifiably wary of giving the self over to unbroken myth, mystical experience, and revealed norms. It may be agreed that all people desire to believe that their chosen life-goals and life-styles are more than merely subjectively valid, that they are in some sense "true." But whether such "truth" can be affirmed in the absence of "faith"—and perhaps even faith which transcends the boundaries of the "empirical"—remains an open question. The Kabbalah and Hasidism asserted that a true way is available for people, and that its rewards are all for which one could possibly hope.

This paper has tried to show that the claims of Jewish mysticism are not fantastic, though the language in which they are articulated may be strange to our ears. For the modern psychologist, indeed for all those who are seeking a path to self-realization in their lives, the kabbalist and the hasid should be seen as partners in an ongoing venture. They offer the conviction that life indeed has meaning, a meaning which directs people to infuse both personal and communal existence with the substance of unification. Even more, they offer the elaboration of this conviction in a concrete pattern for living, one that is religious and mystical, but active and human as well.

References

Buber, M. *Hasidism and modern man.* New York: Harper & Row, 1958.
Buber, M. *The origin and meaning of hasidism.* New York: Horizon Books, 1960.

Buber, M. *Tales of the hasidim: The early masters.* New York: Schocken Books, 1961. (Originally published, 1947.)

Dresner, S. *The zaddik: The doctrine of the zaddik according to the writings of Rabbi Yaakov Yosef of Polnoy.* New York: Schocken Books, 1974. (Originally published, 1960.)

Frankl, V. *Man's search for meaning: An introduction to logotherapy.* New York: Washington Square Press, 1963.

Jacobs, L. *Hasidic prayer.* New York: Schocken Books, 1973.

Krakovsky, L. *Kabbalah: The light of redemption.* Brooklyn: The Kabbalah Foundation, 1950.

Minkin, J. *The romance of hassidism.* North Hollywood, California: Wilshire Book Company, 1971. (Originally published, 1935.)

Rabinowicz, H. *The world of hasidism.* London: Valentine Mitchell, 1970.

Scholem, G. *Major trends in jewish mysticism.* New York: Schocken Books, 1961.

Scholem, G. (Ed.). *Zohar: The book of splendor.* New York: Schocken Books, 1963. (Originally published, 1949.)

Scholem, G. *On the kabbalah and its symbolism.* New York: Schocken Books, 1965.

The Talmud (18 vols.) I. Epstein (Ed.). London: Soncino Press, 1961.

Hasidism, Faith, and the Therapeutic Paradox

Judah C. Safier

The role of the rebbe or zaddik, as illustrated in the folklore of Hasidism (e.g., Buber, 1947; Wiesel, 1972), has been that of moral instructor or examplar. Hasidism was born in southeastern Poland in the middle of the eighteenth century and aimed at restoring the cleavage that had arisen between the scholarly and the masses. The framework of Jewish authority had been shaken by a series of massacres and false messiahs which had left Polish Jewry in a tenuous position, both physically and spiritually. Into this breach stepped the first of the hasidic masters, Rabbi Israel Baal Shem Tov. Helt that Jewish law and learning had been estranged from the realm of everyday life, leading to a separation between Jew and God. He infused the traditional teachings with certain mystical elements which provided a new outlook in religious and social behavior. Through his charismatic leadership, the Baal Shem Tov showed the people how to serve God out of love and joy, rather than out of fear.

The Baal Shem Tov and the zaddikim who followed him offered to their disciples a way of re-awakening the "sparks" which bound them to their Creator. Through that relationship, their followers could find the strength to transcend the mundane realities of their lives. The zaddik provided the inspiration, through formal instruction, example, parable, or song. He showed his hasidim how to find within themselves and through the man-God relationship purpose and direction beyond that which daily life offered.

Insofar as the rebbe's instruction and the relationship he offered helped guide this search for meaning, he may be seen in a light similar to that of the present-day existential-humanistic psychotherapist who, in the therapeutic work, creates the atmosphere within which a seeker (client or "hasid") can try to find a meaningful life-orientation. Kopp (1972) has used the rebbe or zaddik as a metaphor for the therapist, and has found in the hasidic folklore certain parallels to the global therapeutic process. This article will examine Hasidism as an *instructive* process, with a view toward illustrating the "therapeutic paradox" (Haley, 1963; Watzlawick, Beavin, & Jackson, 1967) as it appears in Hasidism.

The first section of this article will describe and illustrate the dynamics of paradox, with specific reference to the implication of paradoxical communication in the etiology of schizophrenia. The second section will discuss the uses of paradox in psychotherapy. These two sections will establish the framework for the third, which will illustrate the uses of paradox in Hasidism. From there, the final section will discuss the role of paradox in the maintenance of faith and the perpetuation of Jewish values.

II

Watzlawick et al. (1967) define paradox as "a contradiction that follows correct deduction from consistent premises" (p. 188). It is a statement or series of statements the outcome of which, arrived at by rationally following the statements, yields an impasse. To clarify the concept, Watzlawick et al. (1967) offer the example of a sign upon which is written: "Ignore this sign." The command is paradoxical in that there is no way that it can be satisfied. To wit: to ignore the sign (i.e., to obey it) one has to see it, which implies that one has not ignored it (i.e., one has disobeyed); if, on the other hand, one chooses to ignore the sign in the first place (i.e., to disobey it), one has, in fact, obeyed it. The self-reflexive nature of the communication—the fact that part of the communication is a *meta*-communication, or a communication about the communication—precludes choice.

In this sense, a paradox is qualitatively different from a simple contradiction. In contradiction, there are clearly alternatives. One may choose from among the alternatives and develop a congruent course of action. In paradox, however, there are no alternatives—there is no "right" decision. The only way to "win" is to step out of the paradox by examining the assumptions which support it. The inability to do this, and the resulting "paralysis," is implicated in a communicational approach to the etiology of schizophrenia.

The "double-bind" theory of schizophrenic development (Bateson, Jackson, Haley, & Weakland, 1956) suggests what can happen to a child who is raised in an environment of paradoxical communications. The intensity of the parent-child relationship, the negation of choice, and the child's inability to comment on the paradox have severe implications for the development of a sense of self. Essentially, the child is placed in a situation where a "right" mode of behavior is unavailable. For example, the child is verbally invited to approach the parent, but a meta-communication qualifies and rescinds that invitation. No matter what the child does, the decision taken will be "wrong." Attempts at approaching will threaten the parent's own tenuous sense of self, so that the parent will continue to invite approach while meta-communicating distance, or vice versa. Attempts at distancing will be perceived as hostility, but the ensuing invitation to approach will be qualified by a distancing meta-communication. There is no way for the child to satisfy these paradoxical injunctions. The child is punished for correctly perceiving the conflicting communicational and meta-communicational worlds, and the schizophrenic "break" becomes one way of commenting on those discrepancies.

There is a Zen tale which offers a more constructive way of dealing with paradox and which will set the tone for the use of paradox in psychotherapy. In the tale, the Zen master holds a stick over the student's head and says: "If you say the stick is real, I will hit you with it. If you say it is not real, I will hit you with it. If you say nothing, I will hit you with it." Obviously, nothing the student can say—or not say—in that situation will prevent the beating. This is true *so long as the student accepts the assumptions of power* implicit in the student-master relationship. Only by questioning these assumptions can the student find a satisfactory resolution—assuming a beating is undesirable—which entails removing the stick from the master's hand. The student must step out of the situation in order to find a satisfactory course of action. So long as the "rules" are not questioned, no solution is available.

III

Haley (1963) discusses the elements of paradox in psychotherapy, and contends that the posing of these paradoxes makes psychotherapy as intense a relationship as that portrayed in the double-bind. The difference is that in therapy the therapist invites the client to look at the paradox, to step out of the situation by questioning the assumptions which support the paradox, and to find a new nonparadoxical way of relating to one's world.

The meta-theory of psychotherapy has certain paradoxical qualities. The client is asked to manifest in therapy the symptomatic behavior which motivated the search for treatment—that is, to change, one must not change, for change implies that the problematic behavior is no longer problematic and, hence, that psychotherapy is unnecessary. Furthermore, the client is asked to place that symptomatic behavior under the therapist's control—in Haley's terms, to "be spontaneous," which is itself a paradoxical command. Finally, the client is told that the search for self-direction and the attainment of *individual* meaning must be undertaken in the context of another person—the therapist.

Both Haley (1963) and Watzlawick et al. (1967) offer multiple examples of paradox in the work of therapy itself. Several illustrations follow:

1. A client repeatedly attempts to dominate the therapist. The therapist says to the client, "Dominate me." If the client proceeds, the client is following the therapist's dictum, and is therefore being submissive. If the client submits, the domination is ipso facto done away with.

2. A disruptive family member is requested by the therapist to be disruptive. Subsequent disruption is then under the therapist's control; the alternative—quiescence—allows the work of therapy to continue unfettered.

3. A couple who seek help because of their arguing are told that the more they argue, the more they are in love (i.e., they must care deeply for each other to argue so much). If they believe the therapist, they will feel more positively toward each other; if they disbelieve, and stop arguing just to prove the therapist wrong, they will again get along better.

Given that there are these paradoxical elements in psychotherapy, how can constructive change and growth result?

The answer lies in the fundamental distinction between the

therapeutic paradox and the one offered in the double-bind. In the therapeutic paradox, another party—the therapist—is present to offer a new way of conceptualizing the situation, which is based on transcending its paradoxical elements. The client is invited to step out of the problematic context and attain a new perspective on it by questioning the assumptions which support the system. The system itself is ostensibly too powerful and of long standing to be changed from within. As in the Zen tale, stepping out of the system changes the "rules," and hitherto unavailable modes of response become available.

This dynamic is illustrated most cogently in the following tale of the Maggid, Rabbi Dov Ber of Mezeritch:

> A farmer and his wife pleaded with him to intercede on their behalf: "We are childless; we want a son."—"Very well," said the Maggid. "That will be fifty-two rubles (fifty two being the numerical value of *Ben,* the Hebrew word for son)." The couple bargained, offered half. To no avail. The Maggid would not budge: "You want me to pray for you? Then you must pay the price." Finally the peasant became angry, and turning to his wife, he said: "Let's go home, we'll manage without him, we'll say our own prayers and God will help us without charge!" "So be it," the Maggid said, and smiled. (Weisel, 1972, p. 73)

In this instance, the assumption underlying the couple's request was that only the zaddik could be instrumental in achieving their goal. The maggid structured the situation in such a way that this assumption was broken, by taking that "symptom" under his control and actually exacerbating it. This created the atmosphere within which the couple could, or was "forced," to transcend their constricting assumption and find within themselves the capabilities which they had previously ascribed to the maggid. Change was facilitated by the maggid's cultivating and working with the "symptomatic behavior" by creating a context within which the assumptions supporting that behavior were untenable; only then could the couple realize their "alternative."

IV

The acceptance of symptomatic behavior, with a view toward the creation of a context where change is possible, was understood by Rabbi Wolfe of Zbaraj:

> People came to him to denounce some Jews who were playing cards late into the night. "And you want me to condemn them?" he cried out. "Why me? And in the name of what? And for what crime? They stay up late? It's a good thing to resist sleep! They concentrate on the game. That is

good too! Sooner or later they will give up card-playing—what will remain is a discipline of body and mind. And this time they will place it in
the service of God! Why then should I condemn them?" (Wiesel, 1972, p.
51)

This story illustrates why the use of paradox in Hasidism and
therapy offers an attractive approach to working with problematic behavior. Attempts at forcing change are often met by resistance, which
introduces a further obstacle to the therapeutic work. The therapeutic
paradox accepts the symptomatic behavior, but creates a context
within which it can be put to more productive ends. It draws on the
client's or hasid's strengths, so that when the problem-supporting context is transcended, these strengths remain to be utilized in the service
of growth.

Other tales illustrate how paradox was actively cultivated by the
hasidic masters. It is told of Aharon of Karlin that

One day he was heard crying: "There are two possibilities. Either God is
king of the world and I am not doing enough to serve Him, or He is not,
and then it is my fault." (Wiesel, 1972, p. 87)

And, in the words of Rabbi Wolfe of Zhitomir:

I fail to understand the so-called enlightened people who demand answers, endless answers in matters of faith. For the believer, there is no
question; for the non-believer, there is no answer. (Weisel, 1972, pp.
87–88)

Both tales present paradoxical situations. For Rabbi Aaron, either
perspective resulted in a heightened religiosity; for Rabbi Wolfe, either
outlook led to a never-ending quest for knowledge. Whatever approach
the hasid took, the result was the same—an increased sense of identity
and oneness with the Divine.

The zaddik also used paradox to establish that the search for God is
itself a significant and worthwhile task. A disciple tells Rabbi Mendel
of Kotzk his woes.

"I come from Rizhin. There, everything is simple, everything is clear. I
prayed and I knew I was praying; I studied and I knew I was studying.
Here in Kotzk everything is mixed up, confused; I suffer from it, Rebbe.
Terribly. I am lost. Please help me so I can pray and study as before.
Please help me to stop suffering." The Rebbe peers at his disciple in tears
and asks: "And who ever told you that God is interested in your studies
and your prayers? And what if He preferred your tears and your suffering?" (Wiesel, 1972, p. 235)

The student is left with the sense that there are no clear answers—that he will never know for certain what is wanted. Rather, each student and each generation must find a set of assumptions which apply to their time and situation. This is a message that is at the core of growth-oriented psychotherapies as well: namely, that *process* is of the essence; stasis is stagnation. The ability to tolerate flux and change, knowing that answers, if they can be found, are often evanescent, is perhaps the most difficult aspect of growth to accept.

As in psychotherapy, the meta-theory of Hasidism is paradoxical as well, as the two following tales will illustrate:

> The mysterious Leib, son of Sarah ... proclaimed to anyone willing to listen: "I came to the Maggid not to listen to discourses, nor to learn from his wisdom; I came to watch him tie his shoelaces." (Wiesel, 1972, p. 61)

Before Rebbe Zusia died, he said:

> When I shall face the celestial tribunal, I shall not be asked why I was not Abraham, Jacob or Moses. I shall be asked why I was not Zusia." (Wiesel, 1972, p. 120)

On the one hand, every aspect of the rebbe's life is to be emulated; on the other hand, one is responsible for developing an independent mode of authentic being. These two approaches appear to be mutually exclusive; and it is in this context that the faith of the hasid is of primary importance. Rabbi Barukh of Medzebozh said:

> To attain truth, man must pass forty-nine gates, each opening onto a new question. Only to arrive finally before the last gate, the last question, beyond which he could not live without faith. (Wiesel, 1972, p. 84)

This is one of the fundamental lessons of Hasidism, and the reason for the establishment in Hasidism of such paradoxical elements. Rationality can take one only to a certain point; maintaining a rational approach beyond that point can eventuate in paradox. The rebbe offered a way of transcending that paradox through the medium of faith, following the supra-rational into areas where rationality could only be destructive and limiting.

This explains the mystical attachment of hasid and rebbe. In the terminology of Bateson et al. (1956), the hasid is involved in an intense relationship which has a high degree of psychological survival value for the hasid. The paradoxical elements within that relationship serve to heighten its intensity. The hasid might well become "double-bound" were there not a socially acceptable way to transcend the paradox. The rebbe represents that way; his offer of relationship is thus an invitation to transcend the paradox which belief can engender.

The hasidic cultivation of paradox, then, is a means of ensuring the existence of a power and mystique within the hasid-rebbe relationship. Living with the hasidic paradox necessitates a leap of faith which enables one to deal constructively with the paradox—by continuing one's search for meaning—without becoming overwhelmed and constrained by it. Insofar as Judaism in general, of which Hasidism is, of course, a sect, similarly has mystical or supra-rational characteristics associated with it, the ways in which Jewish thought has traditionally dealt with paradox should offer some complementary insight regarding the value of paradox in Jewish practice and belief.

V

The survival of Judaism through the ages suggests that the religion defies a strictly rational analysis. While a large focus through the ages has indeed been a rational one—as in the expostulation and codification of the minutiae of Jewish law—there have also developed kabbalistic (i.e., non-rational) elements of practice and belief. Even within the halakhic sphere, the concept of "chok" (statute) illustrates the limits on rationality. Within this context, the existence of paradox in Judaism may serve to illustrate the sources of faith which have enabled Judaism to withstand the onslaught of centuries.

Basically, Judaism has had three ways of dealing with paradox. The strictly legalistic approach has been to search for the "katuv hashlishi"—the third passage that will reconcile two seemingly contradictory passages. Meta-theoretically, this suggests that for every situation there exists an answer. The existence of paradox merely indicates that the answer has not been sufficiently searched for. This approach has ensured the continuity of Jewish outlook through the perpetuation and development of its halakhic framework. In psychotherapy, this approach is represented by a treatment that aims at narrowly-defined symptom-alleviation. The interest is not in underlying dynamics, but in finding an "answer" that will "work."

The second approach has entailed stepping outside the situation to gain a new perspective on it. This approach suggests again that an answer is available, but the means toward finding this answer is in an interpersonal context. Presumably, there exists another person—rebbe or therapist—who can structure the situation so that change is possible. The responsibility for acting on this change, though, resides with the seeker. The most direct parallel in psychotherapy is a client-centered approach. where the creation of the "necessary and sufficient" conditions for change facilitates that process. One's interpersonal relationships are seen as an essential source of support, which would explain why the concept "Kol Yisrael arayvim zeh lazeh" (all of Israel is responsible one for the other) has been of such adaptive value throughout the ages.

The third, "mystical" approach derives from an acceptance of the notion that there may not be any "answers." The Talmud expresses this in the concept of "Tayku," implying that the finite nature of human knowledge and the limitations on human existence preclude the achievement of clearly-defined answers. In this context, the *search* for meaning is seen as primary, and one needs to learn to live with the questions, as answers are not always available. This existential approach characterizes psychotherapists of the "third school," and is ultimately the lesson of Hasidism and Judaism in general.

That lesson is that rationality is not the end-point of existence. Rather, there are paradoxical, non-rational elements of existence which make it intense, powerful, and mystical. Jewish tradition and belief have outlived countless other systems of thought because Judaism has provided a constructive, self-sustaining means of living with these non-rational elements. Faith has provided that outlet, channeling the intense energy generated by paradox into a continuous search for meaning and reinforcing that search as the fundamental component of Jewish existence:

When the great Israel Baal Shem Tov saw misfortune threatening the Jews, it was his custom to go into a certain part of the forest to meditate. There he would light a fire, say a special prayer, and the miracle would be accomplished and the misfortune averted.
Later, when his disciple, the celebrated Maggid of Mezeritch, had occasion, for the same reason, to intercede with heaven, he would go to the same place in the forest and say: "Master of the Universe, listen! I do not know how to light the fire, but I am still able to say the prayer." And again the miracle would be accomplished.
Still later, Moshe-Leib of Sassov, in order to save his people once more, would go into the forest and say: "I do not know the prayer, but I know the place and this must be sufficient." It was sufficient and the miracle was accomplished.
Then it fell to Israel of Rizhin to overcome misfortune. Sitting in his armchair, his head in his hands, he spoke to God: "I am unable to light the fire and I do not know the prayer; I cannot even find the place in the forest. All I can do is tell the story, and this must be sufficient." And it was sufficient. (Wiesel, 1972, pp. 167–168)

In the final analysis, it is the search that is of primary importance. Answers may not always be available, but the questions are significant as well. The hasid could ultimately ask those questions and conduct that search through the telling of the tale. Similarly, the client's telling of the tale—i.e., sharing the existential world with the therapist—paves the way for attainment of meaning. It is the sharing of the tales which makes hasidic and therapeutic encounters interpersonal, intimate, and meaningful.

References

Bateson, G., Jackson, D. D., Haley, J., & Weakland, J. Toward a theory of schizophrenia. *Behavioral Science,* 1956, *1,* 251–264.
Buber, M. *Tales of the hasidim: The early masters.* New York: Schocken Books, 1947.
Haley, J. *Strategies of psychotherapy.* New York: Grune & Stratton, 1963.
Kopp, S. B. *If you meet the Buddha on the road, kill him!* California: Science and Behavior Books, 1972.
Watzlawick, P., Beavin, J. H., & Jackson, D. D. *Pragmatics of human communication.* New York: W. W. Norton, 1967.
Wiesel, E. *Souls on fire: Portraits and legends of hasidic masters.* New York: Random House, 1972.

Discussion: On the Nature of the Therapeutic Encounter Between Hasid and Master

Moshe HaLevi Spero

The conceptualization of the hasid-rebbe relationship as therapeutic, following both the psychoanalytic and the general psychotherapeutic models, has frequented the literature dealing with Hasidism and its relation to psychological values (Applebaum & Metzger, 1976; Gelberman & Kobak, 1963; Safier, 1978; Steindletz, 1960; Woocher, 1978). In particular, Safier (1978) and Woocher (1978) have categorized the rebbe as an existential-humanistic psychotherapist who heals by instruction as well as through the type of relationship he extends toward the hasidic community. In the light of Buber's notion of the dialogical encounter (the "I-Thou" relationship) and his (1957a; 1957b) and others' (Arieti, 1957; Friedman, 1972) attempts to view the ideal psychotherapeutic relationship as such an encounter, it has been intuitively imagined that the hasid-rebbe relationship is surely a similar type of authentic, therapeutic encounter.

While there is no doubt that hasidic teachings and, to some degree, the hasid-rebbe relationship, involve what are called therapeutic elements or effects, the understanding of such elements will vary with the language system or conceptual model one chooses to compare against the phenomena in question. Woocher recognizes this when he states:

> There can be no genuine meeting between modern psychology and religious traditions if the latter are denuded of their specifically "religious" content in order to be assimilated to the former. On the other hand, attempts at language translation can be important as a means of establishing, precisely, that a common framework of concerns *does* exist . . . Once this common agenda of concerns is recognized, it becomes possible to bring the Kabbalah and Hasidism into direct dialogue with important movements in modern psychology. (1978, pp. 33-34)

Obviously, forcing Hasidism into an inappropriate model does not faithfully expand insight into either Hasidism or the model.

A certain precision, then, is called for with the application of modern schema to that which appears to beg for such application within the religious model being examined. The area of concern is three models against which the hasid-rebbe relationship has been compared: general psychotherapy, psychoanalysis, and the I-Thou encounter.

Steindletz (1960), as David Bakan (1958) before him, favored the psychoanalytic model and its apparent relationship to the hasidic master; Applebaum & Metzger (1976), Safier (1978), and Woocher (1978) have been satisfied with more general psychotherapeutic elements seen as inherent in the hasid-rebbe encounter. Buber, of course, considers the hasid-Rebbe relationship an intensely dialogical one.

In fact, psychoanalysis, general psychotherapy, and the I-Thou model are quite distinct types of relationships. Describing the hasid-rebbe relationship as either psychoanalytic, psychotherapeutic, or an I-Thou encounter will entail radically different conceptualizations and says different things about the goals and world-views of this relationship vis-a-vis each model. Some of the uniquely psychoanalytic aspects of the hasid-rebbe relationship, if any exist, will be contradictory to those uniquely dialogical aspects.

II

Summarizing what is generally psychotherapeutic about the hasid-rebbe relationship is not that difficult a task, though it should be noted that the rebbe addressed a class of human maladjustment only recently considered also a legitimate class of problems for psychotherapists to address. This refers to the broad range of so-called existential neuroses—loneliness, alienation, meaninglessness, guiltlessness, anxiety, identity crises and confusion. Though it may be the case that psychotherapy has, as of yet, nothing in particular to offer individuals who suffer, basically, from the human condition itself—and it is obvious that attempts to use psychotherapy as a new type of faith system are not successful (Coles, 1961; Rieff, 1966)—the new humanistic trend is a healthy indication of a widening scope of values on the part of psychology.

There had been those who argued that when the psychologist, and certainly the analyst, is concerned with the patient's views on life, death, and ways of making life meaningful, in a general way, one leaves the realm of "physician" and enters the domain of the moralist or "secular priesthood" (London, 1964; Apolito, 1970). Strictly "psychiatric" problems still exist, yet the most severe pathologies, or the types of problems which would most readily differentiate the rebbe from the psychiatric professional, do not comprise the bulk of problems seen by the average professional in private practice or in community clinics (Howard & Orlinsky, 1972, p. 657).

To be sure, the therapist or rebbe must distinguish between neurotic suffering and everyday misery, but both may rightfully constitute "psychotherapeutic" issues in the modern view. As Wheelis put it, "To get well these days is to get well from loneliness, insecurity, doubt, mistrust, boredom, restlessness, and marital discord" (1958, pp. 40–41). These concerns of the modern psychotherapist were ever those of the hasidic master.

The hasid-rebbe relationship is a therapeutic relationship. This, in itself, is a step toward clarifying whether the hasidic master practiced science or inspiration. That is, one knows of numerous relationships and interactions which are primarily aggravating, destructive, or manipulative, yet which yield some therapeutic outcome for the participants, as in the case of one who forsakes the criminal subculture with fresh attitudes and resolutions about life. Equally, one can think of neutral interactions where therapeutic outcomes were quite fortuitous.

A science of psychotherapy, on the other hand, demands the establishment of a relationship which is purposely structured around and oriented toward the enhancement of psychological growth and well-being. It is this critical element of design which, to the degree that it is evident in the writings and works of the hasidic master, marks the relationship he offered his client as an *essentially* therapeutic one. This relationship may also have been an essentially religious one, but this does not detract from its essential therapeutic aspects since Hasidism may well have conceived of such therapeutic elements as part of an overriding religious world-view.

There are other criteria for a scientific psychotherapy which should be kept in mind; (1) does the therapist have a systematic theoretical grasp of the processes involved in the therapy; (2) can the method be communicated to others, and practiced without the presence of the originator; (3) does the method remain successful after the death of the originator (Kohut, 1971).

III

Psychotherapy research has indicated repeatedly that specific technique of therapy—except in a few, carefully constructed studies—is less relevant as a critical variable of change than certain specific interpersonal factors, such as therapist genuineness, warmth, responsiveness, empathy, unconditional positive self-regard, and others. Frank (1963) stresses that the therapist's influence is due to the distressed patient's perception of the therapist as a source of help. Howard & Orlinsky, following an exhaustive review, stress that

> psychotherapies of all types involve the symbolic communication—through language, gestures, and actions that the patient understands and believes—of benevolent care from a person or agency of respected influence. (1972, p. 659)

Following this definition, the therapist-scientist need primarily pursue these "interpersonal factors" in a systematic way. Applebaum & Metzger (1976), Safier (1978) and Woocher (1978) supply the material which shows convincingly that the hasidic master studied such "interpersonal factors" diligently.

The hasidic rebbe understood, in his own way, that "Psychotherapy is that the vehicle for pursuing goals of symptom relief and positive personality change consists of helping the patient to understand himself better" (Weiner, 1975, p. 18). Said Reb Bunam:

> We are taught that the words of wisdom are "Health to all their flesh" (Proverbs 4:22). This is why Abtalyon said, "Ye sages, be heedful of your words." Since words are as medicine, they must be carefully measured, and precautions taken against their overdose. (Berger, 1910, p. 87)

"Lack of proper understanding is the cause of all tribulations; perfection of knowledge will banish them. . . . The essence of man is his mind and understanding. Hence, what his thoughts are, he is" (Nachman of Bratzlav, 1913, pp. 21–27).

Most unique to this essentially therapeutic relationship was, as Woocher notes, the rebbe's awareness that one must not take over the other's task, rather help the other recognize one's own work and utilize one's own potentials in its performance. Especially in a relationship where the tendency to imitate and emulate the therapist could easily be transformed into a counterproductive "flight into health," the rebbe's ability to foster his clients' independence as soon as possible was a critical therapeutic task.

> Rabbi Shmuel Shiniaver came to Reb Bunam for the first time and introduced himself. Reb Bunam said, "If it is your desire to be a good Jew, your coming was for naught; if you wish to *learn to be* a good Jew, it is well that you have come to me." (cited in Newman, 1963, p. 458)

Karl Jaspers offered three vital aspects of personality needed in a therapist, or in any human being who wishes to live an authentic life. Jaspers (1970) first noted *poise,* or a certain perspective on life, an ability to distinguish things according to their essentiality. The rebbe's perspective was undoubtedly a combination of his halakhic commitments and his hasidic beliefs (e.g., the unity theme stressed in Woocher's essay). Second, the therapist requires *humanitas,* or open-mindedness. This concept involves the ability to put oneself in the other's case and a disinclination to humiliate anyone.

Jaspers noted a third factor: *passion*—an untamed force that must be present as a driving energy to keep the person interested and emotionally invested in the world. According to Safier (1978), part of this force was the rebbe's understanding of "paradox" and his desire to assist his hasidim in dealing with it. Indeed, it was Jaspers who noted that the contemporary therapist must be a philosopher (1964). He said this as an existentialist, but also as one aware of the increasingly complex needs patients were having for the psychotherapist; needs complicated by the existential neuroses previously enumerated. That the psychotherapist could potentially offer more than merely symptom relief was recognized *and proscribed* by Freud (1937/1958). Yet, one must also consider the words of Freud, at age 77: "My discoveries are not a heal-all. My discoveries are a basis for a very grave philosophy of life" (H.D., 1956/1971, p. 25).

IV

It has been shown, in brief, how the hasid-rebbe relationship subscribes to general psychotherapeutic goals, but comparing the hasid-rebbe relationship and psychoanalysis is a more difficult task. In the strictly psychoanalytic model, one no longer discusses general psychotherapeutic terms or even common-sense notions—the *language*

68 The Therapeutic Encounter

of humanistic imagination (Chessick, 1974), but rather the complex mythology, structure, and topography of the psychoanalytic world-view. Psychoanalysis is usually discussed in the *language of scientific understanding;* in terms of cathexes, object-relations, introjects, repression, transference and countertransference, etc. These terms, however, are not an attempt to "fog out" the non-analytic professional, but rather represent a unique attempt to take the elemental phenomenon of the human relationship and submit it to a most rigorous examination.

Steindletz (1960) offers some comparisons between psychoanalytic doctrine and Hasidism. There is a striking similarity between the psychoanalytic requirement that its therapists first be self-analyzed and precursors of this requirement in hasidic thought. First, the notion of "self-analysis" prior to analyzing others is a halakhic requirement. The Talmud notes that one must judge oneself (*keshot atzmechah*) before advising or disciplining others (Talmud, *Sanhedrin*, 18a).

Self-analysis is especially important as a safeguard in a therapeutic process which relies heavily upon empathy as a therapeutic tool. Therapists and rebbes who lack self-awareness tend to interpret what they observe within their own frame of reference, and are consequently handicapped in their efforts to help their clients understand themselves better. Equally important is that the therapist knows what needs are being gratified and which ones are inappropriate to gratify through therapy of another person (Bugental, 1964). As Freud put it so well, "No psycho-analyst goes further than his own complexes and internal resistances permit" (1910/1958, p. 145).

The hasidic master recognized this in the following form; "The Rozdoler Rebbe was asked, 'Wherein does the desire to become a Rebbe differ from other desires?' He replied, 'Before one attains the desire to become a Rebbe, he must break himself of every other desire'" (Berger, 1906/1954, p. 61). The rebbe, like the analyst, has a natural curiosity, but this, too, must be monitored carefully.

Rabbi Enzel of Stry, a noted adversary of Hasidim, once tried to confuse Rabbi Judah Tzvi of Rozdol. He said, "Rozdoler, I am of the belief that the spiritual essence of the Zaddik is an impulsion like all other natural needs of man." The Zaddik answered, "True, but before it can manifest itself it must have subdued all other natural needs." (cited in Newman, 1963, p. 529)

Greenson makes the point that the analytic setting cannot replace the basic psychoanalytic technique—the art of interpretation and the skill in relating to a human being (1967, p. 410). The hasidic master is aware of the power and uses of communication in imparting knowledge to the client. Relating to another human being or the ability to empathize seem intuitively to be matters of technique that should not be particular to any specific type of psychotherapy. Greenson describes what might be involved in relating and empathizing with the patient.

I shift from listening from the outside to listening from the inside. I have to let part of me become the patient, and I have to go through his experiences as if I were the patient, and to introspect what is going on inside me as they occur. (1967, p. 367)

Instructive here is a story related about a previous Lubavitcher Rebbe, Rabbi Dov Ber Schneori, whose custom it was to hear the needs of his individual hasidim, each of whom would leave the rebbe's office with the door ajar signaling the readiness for the next waiting hasid. During one hour, the rebbe's sexton noticed that the door to the rebbe's office had been closed for quite some time while the waiting room filled with anxious hasidim. With some daring, the sexton nudged the rebbe's door open only to find the rebbe lying with his head buried in his hands. As the sexton attempted to inquire, the rebbe sprang up and demanded that the community declare a fast for him and to assemble for afternoon prayers which were to include the services of a fast-day. After the rebbe seemed more calm, R. Pinchas of Shklov inquired of the rebbe's previous behavior. The rebbe answered—the basis by which I can listen to people's problems, sins, and worries is that I can always look into myself and find a disposition for the same problem within me. The last fellow I listened to told me such a heinous story that I could not find any similarity to his life within me. And upon *that* realization, I was mortified, because this only meant that such a similarity did exist but that I had felt the need to repress it (Schachter, 1968, pp. 520a–520b).

It was in such a manner that the hasidic master both empathized with his hasidim as well as scoured the depths of his own personality before taking upon himself the burden of guiding others. Said the Koretzer,

The true Zaddik is always able to see without his eyes and to hear without his ears. A man comes to ask my counsel, and I hear that he himself is telling me, unknowingly, what I should advise him. (cited in Newman, 1963, p. 530)

V

Though there may be other examples of compatibility between psychoanalysis and the hasid-rebbe relationship, it seems that the hasid-rebbe relationship, as well as most generally psychotherapeutic ones, are inconsistent with the basic experiment of psychoanalysis. If it is assumed for the purposes of this argument that both the hasid-rebbe relationship and general psychotherapeutic relationships are interested in and can approximate the I-Thou encounter—a relationship where each participant "means and makes present the other in his personal being . . . where two partners have turned to one another in truth (and) who express themselves without reserve and are free of all desire for semblance" (Buber, 1957b, pp. 111–112)—then they are antithetical to the type of relationship psychoanalysis promotes.

Whether or not psychotherapeutic relationships can be I-Thou encounters is moot, but Buber himself felt that they had the potential to be dialogical encounters and it is clear that many therapeutic modalities aspire to this ideal type of relationship (Spero, 1976). Psychoanalysis, however, could never be such a relationship.

The I-Thou is a relationship without semblance, in Buber's words, or without either partner presenting the self to the other as something or someone the person is not. Yet, the analysand frequently presents various images to the analyst, as the analyst, cloaked in ambiguity, allows the patient to transfer these inappropriate feelings, fantasies, and identities. From the standpoint of the I-Thou, this is semblance. The goal of the dialogical encounter—the encounter of the other as "Thou"—is unnecessary to the analytic program. The type of love which unites the "I" and "Thou" is to be safeguarded in the psychoanalytic setting, where such love would generally be attributed to countertransference. Personhood, in the I-Thou, is a function of an ongoing encounter; in the psychoanalytic situation, personhood is largely a function of the past repeated in the present.

The sense of hope that is experienced in the I-Thou relationship—which serves to call the other ever into response—must, in the psychoanalytic session, be initially repudiated because such hopes are usually based in childhood material and other neurotic fantasies. Though reality based hopes can slowly be encouraged during psychoanalytic work, once they exist they transcend the analysand's relationship with the analyst.

The goal of the psychoanalytic mythology is to take that which is so obviously potent in the phenomenon of the human relationship and to isolate and categorize as many critical components of this phenomenon as would allow the therapist to modulate the intensity, extent, flow, and process of both the therapist's and client's experiences during their relationship. The hasidic rebbe also appreciated the power of the human relationship, yet did not seem interested in so carefully monitoring the process by which it produced results. The I-Thou encounter also accepts the value of whatever transpires between two relating beings without becoming concerned with the processes involved. This is what differentiates the psychoanalytic model of friendship from the hasidic, psychotherapeutic, and I-Thou models.

In this case, when comparing these modes of behavior change, the central focus should be the issue of what purpose did each see for the phenomenon of human relationships. Granted that as methods devoted to behavior change, each, to one degree or another, grasped the fundamentals of psychotherapeutic practice. Yet, they differed in their perspectives on how the therapist relates to a fellow human being. One can consider the hasid-rebbe relationship an essentially therapeutic one, yet one can only consider the hasidic master a psychotherapist in the sense of some models but not others.

The hasid-rebbe relationship tells something about psychotherapy in general; it tells something about one's reaction to crisis at certain historic periods. People today are reacting to crisis by movement away from one's fellows, by increasing bureaucracy, technology, doctrines, daring surgical procedures into the brain, reliance on statistics, and on labels. The hasidic master, relevant to his historic period, sought the commonality of all humankind and a reduction of the inauthentic barriers and narcissistic idols used to isolate people from each other.

Psychoanalysis, in fact, was also an uncovering project, an attempt to expose the basic commonalities shared between suffering and nonsuffering individuals. It recognized that there was a rare value to the closeness between persons and merely attempted to temporarily suspend certain aspects of this closeness for the sake of the therapist and client. Though the hasidic master did not see the need for the creation of such a monolithic "science of friendship," he nevertheless grasped what psychoanalysis was later to grasp about one's need for one's fellow.

VI

In response to whether it is appropriate to consider the hasidic psychotherapeutic endeavor a scientific one, one can state, following Kohut's criteria, that while the rebbe understood some of the processes by which change occurred, there was no systematic psychology presented for this relationship. Second, much of what the rebbe did could be and was communicated to others, yet that which he himself did not understand methodologically could not be transmitted to others. At the same time, those artistic abilities inherent in the hasidic masters which played a role in their success with their hasidim may not have been transmitted as such, but were shared in the sense that one rebbe often understood intuitively what his colleague was doing. The third point is related to the second: does the method remain successful after the death of the originator? Is this an accidental charismatic leadership, or is it replicable science? Part of the answer resides in the fact that Freud was the best Freudian, Adler the best Adlerian, Carl Rogers remains the best Rogerian, etc., even though each of these schools offers students its secrets and methodologies so that they might become Freudians, Adlerians, and Rogerians. That is not to say that psychotherapy stopped after Freud or Adler, but only that a certain creative awareness about human nature such individuals possessed and which they tried to convey to others had to remain essentially related to these individuals' personal characteristics. Similarly, while some of the masters tried to convey their understandings about human nature to others, much of their essential uniqueness remained charismatic.

> The Kobriner visited the Slonimer Rebbe and asked him, "Have your teachers left any writings as a heritage?" "Yes," replied the Slonimer. "Are they printed or are they still in manuscript?" asked the Kobriner. "Neither," replied the Slonimer. "They are inscribed in the hearts of their disciples." (cited in Newman, 1963, p. 241)

Woocher notes that though what the hasidic masters produced were not "scientific" psychologies,

> they do make "empirical" statements about the nature of people and of reality, including Ultimate Reality, and they do prescribe a pattern of human conduct which is designed to respond to the problematics of human existence. (1978, p. 34)

In this sense, much of the rebbe's teachings were incorporated into a single symbolic, if not completely systematized framework which, perhaps, can satisfy the first of Kohut's criteria. More important, however, is the notion that many types of traditions can be scientific in their own ways. One limits understanding of religious traditions and values when comparing them to modern psychological terms and values. On one hand, it is felt that one is interpreting such traditions by these comparisons and analogies, and gives them new meaning. On the other hand, purists maintain that we rediscover through such comparisons the fundamental meanings of science.

At root, people throughout the centuries ask the same questions but seek answers through different frameworks. These frameworks, or *weltanschauungen,* precede one's inquiries even as certain *a priori* assumptions or faiths precede so-called pure scientific inquiry. Thus, even when the responses one seems satisfied with are essentially identical across the centuries, these varying world-views will color, in relative degrees, the terms in which one accepts such responses as valid and relevant.

The modern therapist as clinician and the hasidic master as clinician differed merely in such *weltanschauungen*. To be sure, their talents were often directed toward different types of problems, though it is clear that as the crises of modern individuals increase and fulminate, the modern clinician deals more with issues similar to those "treated" by the hasidic rebbe.

> For some the form of the crisis of values in our time is a religious one: when they have no longer a concept of the Absolute or a sense of divine revelation or belief, they feel shaken. But actually we are all inheritors of this crisis whether we believe or not and whether we care about the question of belief or not. (Friedman, 1974, p. 238)

The "clinicalist" described by Chein (1972), in the desire to comprehend every instance of human behavior in all of its peculiarity and unique individuality, eventually becomes suspicious of every scheme of classification, theory, or statistical evidence. Such an individual rejects probabilities because the very concept abandons the uniqueness of the particular case. Laboratory conditions begin to lose their preeminence as explicators of the human condition. Instead of journals, the insightful therapist begins to feel more secure with the observations and understandings of the great philosophers and poets. Freud was convinced that Dostoevsky was the greatest psychologist of the modern era. One should not be averse to speculating the same of the hasidic masters.

References

Apolito, A. Psychoanalysis and religion. *American Journal of Psychoanalysis,* 1970, *30*(2), 115–123.

Applebaum, S. & Metzger, A. B. Z. Chasidism and psychotherapy: An overview. *Intercom,* 1976, *16*(2), 15–24.

Arieti, S. What is effective in the therapeutic process? *American Journal of Psychoanalysis,* 1957, *17,* 1–25.

Bakan, D. *Sigmund Freud and the jewish mystical tradition.* New York: Schocken Books. 1958.

Berger, I. *Simchat yisroel.* Piotrekov: Grunst, 1910.

Berger, I. *Sepher zechut yisroel.* Jerusalem: Jerusalem Hebrew Book Store, 1954. (Originally published, 1906.)

Buber, M. Distance and relation. *Psychiatry,* 1957, *20,* 91–109.(a)

Buber, M. Elements of the interhuman. *Psychiatry,* 1957, *20,* 110–116.(b)

Bugental, J. F. The person who is the psychotherapist. *Journal of Consulting Psychology,* 1964, *28,* 272–277.

Chein, I. *The science of behavior and the image of man.* New York: Basic Books, 1972.
Chessick, R. *The technique and principles of intensive psychotherapy.* New York: Jason Aronson, 1974.
Coles, R. *The mind's fate: Ways of seeing psychiatry and psychoanalysis.* New York: Little, Brown, and Co., 1961.
Frank, J. *Persuasion and healing.* New York: Schocken Books, 1963.
Freud, S. The future prospects of psycho-analysis. *Standard edition of the complete works of Sigmund Freud* (Vol. 11). London: Hogarth, 1958. (Originally published, 1910).
Freud, S. Analysis terminable and interminable. *Standard edition of the complete works of Sigmund Freud* (Vol. 23). London: Hogarth, 1958. (Originally published, 1937.)
Friedman, M. Dialogue and the unique in humanistic psychology. *Journal of Humanistic Psychology,* 1972, *12*(2), 7–22.
Friedman, M. *The hidden human image.* New York: Delta, 1974.
Gelberman, J. H. & Kobak, D. Psychology and modern hasidism. *Journal of Pastoral Care,* 1963, *17*(1), 27–30.
Greenson, R. *The technique and practice of psychoanalysis.* New York: International Universities Press, 1967.
H. D. *A tribute to Freud.* New York: Oxford Press, 1971. (Originally published, 1956.)
Howard, K. & Orlinsky, D. E. Psychotherapeutic processes. *Annual Review of Psychology,* 1972, *23,* 615–668.
Jaspers, K. *The nature of psychotherapy.* Chicago: Chicago University Press, 1964.
Jaspers, K. *Philosophy* (Vol. 2). Chicago: Chicago University Press, 1970.
Kohut, H. *The analysis of self.* New York: International Universities Press, 1971.
London, P. *The modes and morals of psychotherapy.* New York: Holt, Rinehart & Winston, 1964.
Nachman of Bratzlav (18th Century). *Likkutei etzot hashalem.* Warsaw, 1913.
Newman, L. *The hasidic anthology: Tales and teachings of the hasidim.* New York: Schocken Books, 1963.
Rieff, P. *The triumph of the therapeutic: Uses of faith after Sigmund Freud.* New York: Harper & Row, 1966.
Safier, J. C. Hasidism, faith, and the therapeutic paradox. *Journal of Psychology and Judaism,* 1978, *3*(1), 38–47.
Schachter, Z. *The yehidut: A study of counselling in hasidism.* Unpublished doctoral dissertation, Hebrew Union College, 1968.
Spero, M. H. On the relationship between psychotherapy and judaism. *Journal of Psychology and Judaism,* 1976, *1*(1), 15–33.
Steindletz, E. Hasidism and psychoanalysis. *Judaism,* 1960, *9*(3), 222–228.
The Talmud (18 Vols.). I. Epstein (Ed.). London: Soncino Press, 1961.
Weiner, I. *Principles of psychotherapy.* New York: J. Wiley & Sons, 1975.
Wheelis, A. *The quest for identity.* New York: W. W. Norton, 1958.
Woocher, J. The kabbalah, hasidism, and the life of unification. *Journal of Psychology and Judaism,* 1978, *3*(1), 22–37.

Rabbi Nachman: The Question of His Self-Understanding

James Kirsch

It was Martin Buber who, in his poetic and imaginative publications on Hasidism, singled out Rabbi Nachman of Bratzlav for special consideration (1906/1956). He felt intensive kinship with the stories Nachman told during the last eight years of his life and it was through Buber that Rabbi Nachman became very well known in Western literature. Children as well as adults enjoy his fairy tales. Nachman told these stories in Yiddish but insisted that they be published simultaneously in Yiddish and Hebrew. The Yiddish version became the fountainhead of modern Yiddish literature. Nachman told the stories to his close disciples and Rabbi Nossan of Nemerov was his amanuensis. In his great love and devotion for Nachman, Nossan wrote the stories down as well and as quickly as his excellent memory permitted but he checked every word, not only of the stories but also of the teachings, with Nachman himself. Besides this demanding secretarial activity, he also wrote a biography called *Chaije Moharan*. It is a rather scrambled

but accurate and highly interesting description of Nachman's childhood, teachings, and journeys, which had a messianic purpose.

What makes this biography particularly interesting to a modern
psychologist is that it contains a number of dreams which Rabbi
Nachman had between 1802 and 1810. (He died on October 16, 1810, at
the age of 38.) Nachman himself, and his disciples, considered these
dreams to be divine revelations. Since Nachman considered himself to
have the quality of the Messiah's soul and to be on the same level as
Moses, these dreams had the same significance as Moses' visions for
himself and his small circle of followers.

II

Nachman was the great-grandson of the Baal Shem Tov, the founder
of Hasidism, also called the Besht. Nachman's home was filled with an
atmosphere of great sanctity. But there was something in him which
cannot be explained by the depth of religious devotion in his home,
because as a boy he already lived a secret religious life. When still less
than six years old he loved to go to his great-grandfather's grave and
spend many hours alone there. Even as a child he began to institute
fasts for himself which lasted from one Shabbat evening to the next
Erev Shabbat (eve of Shabbat), in order to gain holiness. He loved to go
to the ritual bath house (*mikvah*). He would spend time there and come
out wet on the coldest night of a Russian winter. Also at six, he was
very well versed in the Bible. He had the usual lessons other Jewish
boys received in those days but he used to beg his teacher always to add
"extra time," and gave him the pennies he could scratch together from
somewhere.

Nachman's personality and extraordinary gifts attracted followers
even before he became *bar mitzvah*—before the age of 13. By then he
had acquired practically all the knowledge available to a Jewish boy in
the Bible, Talmud, and Commentaries. At his *bar mitzvah*, when his
uncle Rabbi Moses Chaim Ephraim of Salidikov examined him, he
was so impressed by his nephew's superior handling of all the examination questions and his profound religiosity that he exclaimed, "He
will be the greatest of the zaddikim."

Under the conditions of Jewish life in Podolia, Nachman took on
what in primitive societies was the function of a shaman. Like every
medicine man, he also had the gift of clairvoyance. One outstanding
example is told in the following story, which has the ring of truth. A
certain man called Shmul Isaac had a long dream which he took quite
seriously and which had very interesting results. The dream was that

he was in some immensely large forest. He could not see any way of getting out
in order to return to his home. He met a man who carried in his belt a sharp
two-edged sword (which is called a *sharfin*) and he (Shmul Isaac) grew very
frightened. But the man showed him a very friendly face and said to him,
"Don't be afraid of me." He went along with the man until they came to a big
house in the forest. There he was told that he would enter this house and that
there would be many small swords hanging, and that he would be allowed to
take some of these small swords, but he should know how to deal with them in
a proper way. He was taken into the house and there an old man was sitting
who said to him, "It is impossible to take *any* sword from there until you
yourself are certain that you are purified from all blemishes on your body and
any infringements of the covenant. Then you will know how to take hold of the
sword that you will take from there."

At this point dark and sinister clouds began to cover Shmul Isaac. Then the
old man pushed him out of the house, saying, "These clouds show that you are
not yet fit enough, but if you will be able to come to a beautiful building in the
forest, *there* is an artisan who sharpens small swords—he even sharpens the big
sword of the man whom you saw and who knows well how to take hold of the
sword. Nevertheless, from time to time he has to have his own sword shar-
pened by this artisan. But who knows whether the artisan will open his door
for you and take you into his house. (Nachman of Bratzlav, 1961, p. 81–82)

All this occurred in the dream, after which Shmul Isaac awoke ter-
rified, his heart pounding furiously. He immediately concluded that he
must bring this matter to Nachman. He walked the great distance
from Dashiv to Slotopolia on foot, although it was the Russian winter.
When he arrived in Slotopolia, he had difficulties in finding
Nachman's house. Finally, he came to Nachman's house, but the door
was closed. He knocked many times until he heard a "still, small voice"
(*I Kings,* 19:12) from behind the closed door. It was Nachman, saying to
him, "You are Shmul Isaac. At present there is no possibility what-
soever to open the door for you." Shmul Isaac stood there for about an
hour and wept loudly with a broken heart. Then Nachman opened the
door for him and said,

Didn't they tell you still in your house "Who knows whether you will be
able to enter? I realized that all gates would be closed. But the Gate of
Tears, which you have wept, is not closed." (1961, p. 82)

Then Shmul Isaac understood that Nachman knew about his dream,
but he was afraid to tell him so. But then Nachman said to him, "Didn't
many clouds surround you?" He was amazed and astonished about the
holy spirit in Nachman; still he could not open his mouth to say
anything—not even one word—to Nachman about his dream.
Nachman's detailed knowledge of Rabbi Shmul Isaac's dream is certainly evidence of his clairvoyance, but it also demonstrates what im-

portance hasidic Jews attributed to dreams in those days. Nachman
even considered it as a blessing if he appeared in the dreams of his
followers.

III

Since Nachman was so profoundly versed in the Hebrew Bible, it is
no wonder that biblical figures, whole biblical verses, or outstanding
visions appeared in his dreams. One cannot always see why Nachman
considered his own dreams to be revelations. The use he made of his
own dreams was totally different from the way one interprets them
today. The psychological viewpoint simply did not exist for Nachman.
He never considered the possibility the dream might convey a criticism
of him or compensate his conscious attitude.

There is one dream that has drawn the attention of several interpreters. Nachman told the dream to his followers in November of 1809.

I was sitting in my house. (Nossan adds: "in the small house in which he
lived"). No one was brought into me. That was quite astonishing to me so I
went out into the next room. No one was there either. Then I went out to the
Beth Ha'Midrash (house of study) and again there was no one there. So I made
up my mind to go outside, and I *did* go outside. There I saw that many men
were there, huddled together in circles and whispering one to the other. One
was scoffing at me, and another was laughing at me. Still another was very
contemptuous of me, and so on. Even my own followers were against me. Some
of them also treated me with contempt, others whispered secretly against me,
and so on. I called to one of my followers and asked him, "What is all this?" He
answered, "How could you do something like that? How could you commit a
great sin like that?" But I didn't know at all why they were scoffing at me.
Therefore I asked this particular man to go and assemble some of my followers.
He went away, and I did not see him anymore. I thought to myself: what should
I do now? I considered running away to some other country. So I did—but there
it was the same thing. Some men were also standing around, talking about me,
knowing the same thing. So I considered going into some forest, where I would
gather to myself five of my followers. I went with them into the forest and we
stayed there. Since we needed something—food and other things—we sent one
of our own men to buy us what we needed. I asked him whether the turmoil had
calmed down and he answered, "No, the turmoil is still very strong."
    While we were sitting there an old man came along. He called me and said
he had something to talk to me about. I went with him and he began to talk
with me. He said, "How could you do a thing like that? Aren't you ashamed
before your fathers, before your grandfather, Rabbi Nachman (Horodenko),
and before your great-grandfather, the Besht? And aren't you ashamed before
the Torah of Moses and the Holy Fathers, Abraham, Isaac and Jacob? What do
you think?—that you will just sit here? Can you sit here forever? And will your
money last you forever? You are only a weak man. What will you do? Do you
think you can take off to any country? Whatever you do, and in any event—if

they don't know there who you are, then you cannot live there because they will not give you money, and if they *do* know who you are, you also could not stay there because there they would soon know about this."

I answered him, "If it is so that I am such an outcast, then I would still have the *Olam Habo* (the world to come)." He answered, "You really believe you will have the world to come? Not even in Hell (*Gehenna*) will you find any place to hide, because you have done such a terrible thing. I answered him, "Go away. I thought that you would comfort me and speak to my heart. Instead you give me afflictions. Go away." The old man went away from me.

While I was sitting there I thought to myself: since I am sitting here such a long time I could completely forget everything I have learned. I told the man whom we had sent into the city for our needs that he should ask there for any book and bring it to me. He had gone into the city but he did not bring back a book. He said it was impossible to bring it because it surely was forbidden to reveal for whom one needed the book and it was impossible to find the book clandestinely. I suffered greatly because I was "a fugitive and a vagabond" (Cain's expression in *Genesis* 4:14). I had no book at all and I could forget all my learning.

After this the old man returned again, carrying a book under his arm. I asked him, "What are you carrying?" He answered, "A book." I said to him, "Give me the book!" and he gave it to me. I took it, but I did not even know how to set the book down. I opened the book but I didn't understand anything in it. It appeared to me to be in an alien, strange language and in a strange script, because I could make nothing of it at all. It upset me very much. I was afraid that once those men who were with me became aware of this they might desert me.

At this moment the old man called me and wanted to talk to me, so I went with him. Again he began to speak in the same fashion: "How could you do a thing like that? Aren't you ashamed? Not even in *Gehenna* will there be a place where you can hide." I said to him, "If any man from the Higher World would speak to me like that I would believe him." He answered, "I *am* from there." And he showed me something (to prove that he was a being from the Higher World). At this moment I remembered the wellknown story of the Besht—that at that time the Besht also thought he would not have a part in the world to come, but said: "I love God, the Almighty (even) without the world to come." And I threw my head back in utter anguish like this, there came and gathered around me all the men who were mentioned before, and those before whom the old man had told me to be ashamed, namely my grandfather, the patriarchs, and the others. And they spoke to me the following verse:

And the fruit of the land excellent and comely
For them that are escaped of Israel. (*Isaiah,* 4:2)

And they said to me, "On the contrary, we are glorified by you." Then they brought me all my followers and my own children (because my children had also deserted me in the beginning). They spoke to my heart words which were the opposite of what they had said in the beginning. All this because I threw my head back! They said even if there was a man who transgressed upon the whole Torah eight-hundred times—if he threw his head back in bitterness like this, they would surely forgive him. I don't want to tell you the rest of the good things they said, because I do not want to boast to you. (Nachman of Bratzlav, 1962, p. 42–43)

IV

The late Joseph G. Weiss analyzed this dream in a Hebrew article. Although there are some interesting points in his analysis, it suffers from a basic misunderstanding about the nature of dreams. He deals with the dream as if it had been a real event and not an utterance of the unconscious. This ignorance of modern psychological research permeates his entire article. The title of his article, "Rabbi Nachman of Braslav on the Controversy Concerning Himself," is already misleading. The dream has nothing to do with the controversies Nachman was involved in with other zaddikim but describes an inner conflict, since all dreams are a self-representation of the psyche. Nevertheless, Weiss does see that Nachman's self-understanding and the question of identity are the central problems in this dream. For example, he says:

> Nachman summarized the self-understanding of his life as it was crystallized in the order of the coordinates of feeling of shame and of consciousness of guilt.... The question of identity rises and breaks out of Nachman's struggles with guilt and out of his struggles with shame. (1967, pp. 101; 105)

However, it is not Nachman who summarizes the self-understanding but the unconscious which does it. This distinction between ego and unconscious might appear irrelevant but in practice it quite often makes the difference between a psychosis and a neurosis. In Nachman's case, it is of the greatest importance because he tended to identify with the soul of the messiah, an archetypal image which caused him to make presumptuous statements about himself.

Furthermore, Weiss identifies the old man in the dream as Rabbi Arje Leib of Shpole, who, according to Weiss, "organized" Nachman's persecution, while the dream clearly identifies the old man as a man from the "Higher World"—in Jung's psychological language, an archetype.

Arthur Green also mentions this dream in his article, "Rabbi Nachman Bratzlaver's Conflict Regarding Leadership," in which he says that "States of elation and depression would sometimes alternate for Nachman within minutes" (1975, p. 152). This is characteristic for psychogenic depression, and Green himself follows this with two paragraphs of excellent description of Nachman's periods of elation and depression. He feels this dream is particularly instructive for understanding Nachman's depressions. He further says:

> Pervading the dream most basically is an overwhelming sense of guilt. The real cause of Nachman's suffering is an unbearable burden of guilt,

an unyielding awareness of his own sinfulness . . . From countless other passages in the literature of Bratzlav, it becomes quite clear that the sense of sin which constantly oppressed Nachman was that very sin which he had claimed to have overcome altogether: sexual desire. (1975, p. 155)

In his conscious life Nachman felt all types of appetite (ta'avoth), especially sexual desires, were sinful. He tried to overcome them and even boasted that he had overcome all of them. In fact, the dream never mentions sexuality directly or in a symbolic way. Dreams are compensatory, and since Nachman was so conscious of sexuality it is most improbable that the unconscious would deal with sexuality. The question which must have carried a great deal of weight for Nachman was his illness, the tuberculosis which was taking its fatal course. Nachman knew at the time of this dream that he would die in the foreseeable future. The writer's experience as a psychotherapist confirms that in *conspectu mortis* the unconscious presents a person with an overview of one's life, and its value and achievements.

V

According to Jung, the first part of any longer dream states the subject of the dream. The dream begins with a situation which practically never occurred in Nachman's conscious life, namely that he "was sitting alone in his house," because it appears that in real life his servant or some of his disciples were with him at all times. In the dream he goes outside and sees many men huddled together in circles. Within these circles the people are whispering one to the other, scoffing at him, laughing at him, being contemptuous of him. The circular arrangement indicates that he was confronted with the self. The circle, or mandala, is a symbol of the self, as Jung has demonstrated in many places in his books (1959, p. 355-384). Therefore, *the subject of the dream can only be Nachman's relationship to the self*. It is alive as a "multitude of voices." It is roused against the dreamer. The overwhelming sense of guilt that Green speaks about deals with this relationship to the self. A dialogue begins between the ego, Nachman, and the figures, components of the self. Nachman asks, "What is all this?" and he is told in a mysterious way that he had committed a "great sin." He is quite unconscious of what sin it could be and he is not given any direct answer. He tries to run away from the problem, thinking that he can escape into some forest with perhaps "five of his followers." And so he does. Being removed from important human aspects of the self, he discovers that the "turmoil," the disturbing hostile emotion in the self, continues to be strong.

At this point an old man comes along. As we hear later, he is a man from the other world. In our language, he is the archetypical Old Wise Man. Jung has given an extensive description of this archetype (1953, p. 94–95). He appears quite frequently as a prefiguration of the self. Here he speaks as the voice of conscience. He begins a thorough examination of Nachman's basic relationship to himself and to God. The old man brings up the question of Nachman's sin. He reminds Nachman of his grandfather and the patriarchs, the holy fathers of the Jewish people. In other words, he confronts Nachman with his tradition and the many incarnations of the Old Wise Man figure in Jewish history. He convinces Nachman that he cannot escape from his problem by running away to other countries. Nachman responds by saying that although he might be an outcast in *this* world he still will have his portion in the "world to come." Then the old man says the terrible thing—that even in the world to come, in the after-life, there will be no place where Nachman can hide, not even "in the deepest of hells, *Gehenna*," because, as the text says, Nachman has done "something very bad" (*hillul haShem*) (Nachman of Bratzlav, 1962, p. 42). As this term is used in Yiddish it has lost its original meaning of blasphemy and has been reduced to meaning something very bad. One could argue that something of the original meaning might still have been present in Nachman's mind when he dreamt this dream. I understand this crucial line as leaving Nachman still in a quandary as to what the nature of his sin is. The words might contain a hint that the sin is of religious nature and might be compared to blasphemy in its severity of sinfulness.

Nachman certainly does not betray any feeling that his sin might have been blasphemy. He is simply disappointed that the old man did not comfort him and did not speak to his heart in his extreme isolation. So he brashly sends the old man away. Like Job, Nachman's conscious viewpoint is that he has committed no sin. Job says:

When I say: "My bed shall comfort me,
My couch shall ease my complaint,"
Then thou scarest me with dreams,
And terrifiest me through visions.
(Job, 7:13–14)

VI

The central problem in this dream is Nachman's sin. Right at the beginning it is stated that there is a turmoil of contempt and scoffing directed against him in the circle of his men. Another indication of his unconscious guilt is his attempt to run away. Finally, there is the old man's statement.

In psychological terms, that statement indicates that there must be an outspoken difference between Nachman's image of God and the one the unconscious presents him with. One cannot know what God is but the organs of the human psyche form an image of the *ens ineffabile*. We cannot identify the psychological fact, the archetype of the self, with God, but it has been observed in modern times that the *image* of the self and the image of God frequently coincide (Jung, 1958, p. 156).

In the first interval between the old man's visits Nachman realizes that his isolation is not only local but also spiritual. He discovers that he is completely stripped of all the knowledge he has learned from the books. To correct this he sends one of his men out into the city for a book but the man returns without it. This is reminiscent of a statement made by the alchemist Geber, quoted by Jung: "libros rumpite, ne corda vestra corrumpantur" (tear up the books, lest your hearts be corrupted) (1954, p. 272). The unconscious evidently deprives Nachman of all book-learning in order that he can receive the knowledge the unconscious has for him.

When the old man reappears he brings a book with him which has all the knowledge of the unconscious, but Nachman, with his far-fetched and outlandish kabbalistic associations, is so far from all the knowledge of the unconscious, the *lumen naturae* as the alchemists called it, that he cannot make anything of it. The occurrence of a foreign language, which the dreamer does not know at all, is a very frequent motif in dreams of modern people. Nachman calls the symbolic language of the unconscious "a strange, alien language in a strange script." One sympathizes with Nachman, whose understanding of the language of the unconscious was blocked by his kabbalistic training and a surfeit of book-learning.

The old man comes to Nachman a third time and wants to talk to him. He addresses Nachman and tells him again that there is no hiding-place for him anywhere, not even in *Gehenna* would he find a place where he could hide. This image of the lonely ego exposed to the powers of hell reminds one of the terrible tortures to which the human being is exposed in the after-death state in the Tibetan Book of the Dead.

Then the Lord of Death will place around thy neck a rope and drag thee along; he will cut off thy head, tear out thy heart, pull out thy intestines, lick up thy brain, drink thy blood, eat thy flesh, and gnaw thy bone; but thou wilt be incapable of dying. Even when thy body is hacked to pieces, it will revive again. The repeated hacking will cause intense pain and torture. (Evans-Wentz, 1957, p. xlvii)

These stark images of torture in the after-death state should be taken as symbols of spiritual torment. Since Nachman does not understand the language of the unconscious and its psychological meaning, he avoids such suffering in *Gehenna,* but it is at this point that the old man reveals himself as a man from the "Higher World." In this desperate situation, Nachman affirms his love of God and, as an expression of his love, and his bitterness at being so utterly alone, he throws back his head in anguish. It is this love of God which overcomes his utter loneliness and now brings back his grandfather, the patriarchs, and all the others, and they speak to him a few words from *Isaiah.* The reason that this line (only a part of the verse), out of the many thousands of verses which Nachman knew by heart, appears in the dream can only be guessed at. The whole verse is:

In that day shall the growth of the Lord (God) be beautiful and glorious.
And the fruit of the land excellent and comely
For them that are escaped of Israel. (*Isaiah,* 4:2)

It has found many interpretations. Literally, the land will yield rich produce. Others regard it as symbolic of the Messiah or the righteous who survived the day of wrath. Since Nachman was convinced that his soul was akin to the soul of the Messiah, or was even a portion of the Messiah's soul, he must have understood this line as messianic symbolism. It must have meant to him that he was one of Israel's survivors and that he would therefore receive the fruit of his work, the fulfillment of our messianic hopes. By quoting this line from *Isaiah* his ancestors reconnect him with his followers and his sons, and they reestablish his wholeness, not in the sense of integrating the unconscious or the self, but in the sense of reconnecting him completely with his ancestors and Jewish tradition in general. They exclaimed that even if a man would have transgressed the (commandments of) Torah 800 times and still threw his head back in bitterness, they surely must forgive him. The time was not yet ripe for Nachman to undergo the tortures of meeting the self, of finding wholeness and bringing a truly new message to the Jewish people.

VII

It is of great importance to realize that this dream represents a general accounting of Nachman's life. Although he did not achieve individuation, the work he did, and the love of God which filled him, made him an inspiring teacher for the Jewish people. From the viewpoint of individuation he failed but from the viewpoint of Jewish tradition and all its great values, his life was a great success. Dreams containing so much conflict about one's whole life work are characteristic at the end of one's life. Nachman in a very short time had achieved very much and had done everything to bring holiness into his life.

The "sin" which was never named in the dream could not have been sexual in nature because Nachman was very conscious about all types of concupiscence, including sexual desirousness. It was psychological in nature. In layman's terms, it was his aggrandizement. His profound conviction that he was of the same stature as Moses, Rabbi Yitzchak Luria, and the Besht, contrasted sharply with his pronounced assertion of humility before God. In psychological terms it was his identification with the self, which fortunately was not complete. Otherwise, he would not have been a saint but a psychotic. He was saved from such a dire fate by the fact that throughout his life Nachman paid great attention to his dreams and considered them a direct revelation from God. It was only natural that in the course of his life the unconscious would present Nachman with a natural image of God or, as Jung preferred to say, a natural image of the archetype of the self. Any distance of alienation from the image of the self is experienced as guilt. Sin was not understood in this dream as a violation of the traditional image of God but as an alienation from the archetype of the self. In Nachman's day there was no possibility to understand such things. It is very comforting to know that in the end the dream released Nachman from that tragic conflict and comforted him with the voices of his ancestors, fathers, and children.

References

Buber, M. *The tales of Rabbi Nachman.* New York: Horizon Press, 1956. (Originally published, 1906.)

Evans-Wentz, W. U. *The tibetan book of the dead.* London: Oxford University Press, 1957.

Green, A. *Texts and responses.* Leiden: E. J. Brill, 1975.

The Holy Scriptures (2 vols.). Philadelphia: Jewish Publication Society, 1917.

Jung, C. G. *Two essays on analytical psychology.* New York: Pantheon Books, 1953.

Jung, C. G. *The practice of psychotherapy.* New York: Pantheon Books, 1954.

Jung, C. G. *Psychology and religion.* New York: Pantheon Books, 1958.

Jung, C. G. *The archetypes and the collective unconscious.* New York: Pantheon Books, 1959.

Nachman of Bratzlav. *Nachal Novea.* Jerusalem: Yobel, 1961.

Nachman of Bratzlav. *Chaije Moharan* (Part 2). Jerusalem: Vardi, 1962.

Weiss, J. G. Rabbi Nachman of Braslav on the controversy concerning himself. In E. E. Urbach, R. J. Zwi Werblowsky & C. Wirszubski (Eds.), *Studies in jewish mysticism and religion.* Jerusalem: Magnes Press, 1967.

Extended Consciousness and Hasidic Thought

Nathan Kuperstok

It was the counterculture of the last decade which provided the challenge to the idea that the technocratic rationality associated with mechanistic science is the only valid way of knowledge. Science was indicted for having denatured personal experience by removing life's mystery and sacredness (Roszak, 1969), and instead of knowledge obtained from the quantifying "objective" method associated with positivism and empiricism, the counterculture developed an epistemology centering around direct sensuous experience, intuition and subjectivity (Blackburn, 1974). The conceptual-abstract, rational, logical, and verbal approach to reality was relegated to secondary status. More important valence was attached to non-rational, transcendent experience, with the conviction that the intellect or reason, seen as only one component of the mind, was actually screening from awareness other kinds of knowledge. The stultifying vision of the reality created by the Western person did not seem to bring fulfillment. Vast numbers of people turned to psychedelic drugs, meditation, various religious cults and disciplines in an attempt to explore inner reality, extend awareness, and achieve alternative lifestyles open to spiritual knowledge.

There was a shift in the field of psychology which paralleled, and to some extent contributed to, the counterculture. Humanistic psychology, known as the Third Force and strongly influenced by Maslow, developed with its emphasis on self-actualization and peak experiences. Soon, the rapidly growing "human potential" movement led to many shades of "human growth" experts emphasizing authenticity, freedom, love, community, joy, creativity, and ego-transcendence, through a myriad of therapies—encounter, t-group, marathon sessions, gestalt, and psychodrama. A Fourth Force emerged, exploring transpersonal experiences and altered states of consciousness, replete with journals and investigators. In particular, the ability to experience new states of consciousness without the use of mind-altering drugs led to a serious study of Eastern disciplines such as Zen and Yoga, called by Ornstein (1972) the esoteric psychologies.

This paper attempts, in an exploratory manner, to show that some of the objectives in Jewish mystical teachings parallel those contained in the esoteric psychologies. For the purposes of this article, the school of Chabad Hasidism is used, as it exemplifies a latter day manifestation of the Jewish mystical tradition.

II

Consciousness is a personal-cultural construct based on a process of selection and limitation. The many-dimensional complexity of any given stimuli constellation is reduced, selected, organized and processed by the senses, the central nervous system, and one's assumptive world. Personal consciousness represents only a small fraction, a tiny abstraction of whatever is "out there."

The transactionalist school in psychology clarified the semi-arbitrariness of perception. From an amorphous, chaotic universe of stimuli, the person constructs an assumptive world which imposes an order and regularity on the impinging welter of experiences. This assumptive world is primarily influenced by the metaphysical beliefs of a given culture and consists of unconscious conceptual abstractions and categories, expectancies, awarenesses, assumptions, biases, needs, and intents, all of which select evidence and interpret perceptions. The result is a consistent model of reality, the consensus reality of a given culture. Sharing the same metaphysical system and hence developing a particular assumptive world, a culture conceptualizes what is "out there" and calls it reality.

However, this consensus reality, because it consists of a shared sys-

tem of perceptions and verbal descriptions, is largely a social conven-
tion. Since perception and one's assumptive world are largely a
personal-cultural construct, other constructs of consciousness, other
models of reality, are possible.

That there is no absolute model of reality against which perceptions
can be measured as true or false is clearly demonstrated by mind-
altering drugs, which interfere with the ordinary way the senses and
central nervous system filter incoming information. Altered consciousness through drug ingestion suggests that the senses and central
nervous system represent things neither wrongly nor correctly, but
that they produce, under different circumstances, different sensations
and perceptions. Carlos Castenada's (1968) hallucinogenic experience,
under the tutelage of Don Juan, led him to see the world in a structur-
ally different way from ordinary vision.

According to LeShan (1974), one way of achieving an altered state of
consciousness is by using a different metaphysical system. By entering
a different metaphysical system, one perceives and reacts to the universe as if it were run on a different set of laws and principles. In
different metaphysical systems, different things are possible. Castenada (1971, 1972) experienced the teaching of a coherent system of
beliefs and found that the non-ordinary reality perceived, the reality of
"special consensus," was utilizable. It could be put into service to
achieve practical results, although the behavior involved in such a
process may seem, to the Western consciousness, irrational and illogi-
cal. Indeed, Tart (1975) argues that different states of consciousness
produce different logics and perceptions. Any logic consists of a basic
set of assumptions and a set of rules for manipulating information
based on these assumptions. An altered state in which the metaphysical and normative assumptions are changed produces a different logic.
"Rational" thinking is contingent on state of consciousness. As Tart
states:

> Rationality is not some absolute, universally valid way of thinking. Ra-
> tional means "according to the rules," but where do the rules come from?
> We now understand that there are many logics, many ways of being
> rational. Each logic has different assumptions behind its rules, and as-
> sumptions are arbitrary. (1975, p. viii)

Reality is thus a state of consciousness, a cultural construct, or,
according to Pearce (1975 a; b), a conceptual framework which changes
from culture to culture and age to age. Our assumptive world, particularly our categories, concepts and needs, to a large extent direct the
perceptions which constitute our reality. Each culture, discipline, or
ideology acts as a prism through which whatever is "out there" is

ordered into a coherent and shared world. A scientific theory in many ways resembles the workings of the assumptive world by controlling the type of observations made, the interpretation of these observations, and the "truth" or "facts" that are accepted. As Einstein once mentioned, theory decides what we observe, not vice versa (Hebb, 1975).

III

At the grossest level of differentiation, consciousness has been found to be not single, but dual. Deikman (1974) attempts to delineate this duality into the action mode and receptive mode, each differing from the other in physiological and psychological manifestations. The action mode, a state organized to manipulate the environment, consists physiologically of sympathetic nervous system activity and involves the striate muscle system, EEG beta waves and increased muscular tension. Psychologically, the action mode produces focal attention, object-based logic and heightened boundary perception. The receptive mode, on the other hand, is a state organized around the intake of the environment. Physiologically, it consists of parasympathetic activity, EEG alpha waves, and decreased muscular tension. Its dominant psychological attributes are diffuse attending, paralogical thought, decreased boundary perception, and sensory experience. The interplay between the two modes accounts for the psychological and physiological variations which occur from minute to minute.

Western society is largely action mode oriented, with language as its essence, enabling one to analyze and divide up the world and thus manipulate it. Its time dimension is future oriented. The "knowing" gained by using the action mode is only one kind of knowledge. Within it one cannot think outside one's language structure (the Whorfian hypothesis). The receptive mode, operating in a present-centered time dimension, plays a major role in meditation, mystical experiences and altered states of consciousness. It provides ways of "knowing" certain aspects of what is "out there," usually non-verbally and inaccessible to the action mode. It addresses itself to reality dimensions other than those associated with logical thinking and the object world.

Recent work on hemispherectomy (e.g., Bogen, 1974; Gazzaniga, 1974; Sperry, 1964), has given biological support for the ancient conception of the duality of consciousness. This duality is found in the right and left hemispheres of the brain, each hemisphere subtending different functions and different modes of information processing. The right hemisphere operates in holistic rather than analytic mentation, processing information diffusely and integrating many aspects at once.

It has limited language ability and works largely through intuition, primarily responsible for music, arts, crafts, orientation in space, body image, and perhaps mystical experiences. Its time conceptualization is that of present-centeredness. The left hemisphere processes information linearly, sequentially, operating through analysis, discrimination, reason, logical thinking and language. It conceptualizes time as past, present, and future.

Although the two modes complement each other, cultures differ in their relative predominance. For example, Dorothy Lee (1974), studying the Trobriander tribe, found that they apprehended reality largely through the right hemisphere. Their consciousness is one of present centeredness and nonlinearity. For them, there is no temporal connection between events, no tenses, no distinctions between past and present. What to the Western person is a causal relationship in a sequence of connected events is to the Trobriander an ingredient in a patterned whole.

Both modes of conceptualizing reality are equally valid. They consist of different types of consciousness and lead to different models of reality. The western world has been largely dominated by left hemispheric consciousness. Its extreme veneration as being the only mode to apprehend whatever is "out there" has been an important point of contention in the counterculture revolution.

Consciousness, therefore, is a personal-cultural construction and, in an "ordinary" state, is bimodal. Altered states of consciousness, resulting in different realities, can come about as a result of a qualitative alteration in the overall pattern of mental functioning, a change in the interplay of psychological structures or subsystems (Tart, 1975). The esoteric psychologies consist of a system of techniques which induce a change in ordinary consciousness. The result is a form of extended consciousness, a "truer" reflection of reality.

IV

Jewish mysticism, like other Eastern disciplines, consists of a set of actions, both cognitive and behavioral, which facilitate the development of an extended consciousness.

The Torah (revealed law), as viewed by traditional Judaism, is a coherent, comprehensive metaphysical system, a model of reality. As such, one who relates to the universe as if it were run on Torah principles is, in effect, embracing a particular consciousness which differs from conventional Western consciousness simply because many of the assumptions differ.

The Torah constitutes the law and order of the universe, the blueprint of creation. As the Zohar declares, "God looked into the Torah and created the universe" (Zohar, II, 161a). The Torah is often referred to as light (e.g., *Proverbs,* 6:23). Through the Torah one is able to "see" reality. Just as it is the structure of the universe, so it structures one's consciousness.

God, the Infinite (En Soph), is the Ultimate State of Consciousness. God is a simple unity, which, by definition, is the opposite of differentiation and separateness, and yet includes them. As the Ultimate State of Consciousness, there is no state of consciousness apart from or outside of God, who is absolutely all inclusive, the Ultimate Reality. As the Bible states:

> Unto you it was shown, that you might know, that the Transcendent God is the Immanent God: there is nothing else but Him. (*Deuteronomy,* 45:35)

The school of Chabad emphasizes meditation on God as the absolute reality, so that the idea becomes firmly established in one's consciousness. The Tanya declares:

> Let him then concentrate his mind and envisage in his intelligence and understanding the subject of His blessed true Unity: how He permeates all worlds, both upper and lower, and even this whole earth . . . and how everything is of no reality whatever in His presence; and He is One Alone and the very same in the upper and lower realms, as He was One Alone before the six days of Creation; and also in the space wherein the world was created, the heavens and earth, and all their host—He alone filled this space; and now also this is so, being One Alone without any change whatever. (Tanya I, p. 192)

The Torah, however, as a metaphysical system, is more than just one model of reality. Judaism sees Torah as infinite, containing within it the ultimate model of reality, speaking to people in materialistic, corporeal terms and yet referring to sublime and exalted realities:

> Because the Torah and the Holy One, blessed be He, are one, the meaning of this is that the Torah, which is the wisdom and will of the Holy One, blessed be He, and His glorious Essence are one, since He is both the Knower and the Knowledge. (Tanya I, p. 36)

In effect, the Torah speaks of higher realities, but the person grasps the allusion which relates to lower realities (Likutei Sichos, 2, p. 364).

V

A major obstacle to the development of an extended consciousness is that those portions of the external environment which do not suit one's needs or desires at the moment are tuned out. In order to destructure conventional consciousness and experience other modes, non-attachment to objects and sense pleasures are greatly emphasized in the esoteric psychologies. This renunciation is a process of conquering desires associated with worldly goods and pleasures, and hence removes distractions which interfere with the perception of other aspects of what is "out there." Through renunciation, conventional perceptual and cognitive structures are disrupted so that the receptive mode is able to surface, and aspects of reality previously filtered from awareness because of desires are experienced.

Torah actually structures a way of life containing non-attachment to materialism. This is particularly emphasized by the commandments, especially the many prohibitive ones (You shall not . . .), and included in the principle "Sanctify yourself in things permissable" (Talmud, *Yebamoth,* 20a). Indeed, the Hebrew word "kedusha," denoting holiness and sanctity, implies non-attachment and separation from materialistic reality and its desires (Tanya I, pp. 159–161).

Meditation plays a crucial role in many of the esoteric psychologies as a powerful technique used to destructure conventional consciousness. Ornstein (1972) differentiates two types of meditation. One kind is practiced by keeping external sources of stimulation to a minimum and restricting awareness to a single, unchanging source of stimulation.

Restricting awareness to God's omnipresence, as in "I have placed God before me constantly" (*Psalms,* 16:8), is an essential feature of Judaism. Chabad emphasizes set periods during the day for meditating on God, a process called reflective meditation by Assagioli (1973). This serves as an exercise to cleave or attach oneself to God, and to ideogenically generate appropriate emotions. Attachment to God is the corollary of non-attachment to materialistic desires and needs.

> For when the intellect in the rational soul deeply contemplates and immerses itself exceedingly in the greatness of God, how He fills all worlds and encompasses all worlds, and in the presence of Whom everything is considered as nothing—there will be born and aroused in his mind and thought the emotion of awe for the Divine Majesty . . . Next his heart will glow with an intense love, like burning coals, with a passion, desire and longing, and a yearning soul, towards the greatness of the blessed In-

finite... of which Scripture speaks as "My soul longeth, yea, even fain-
teth." (Tanya I, p. 32)

The Tanya adds:

to rule the heart by means of meditation in the mind on the greatness of
the blessed Infinite, whereby his understanding will beget... fear of the
Lord ... and the love of God ... with a fervor and desire to cleave to Him
through the fulfillment of the precepts. (Tanya I, pp. 99–100)

In the end result,

his soul will spontaneously be kindled and it will ... willingly lay down
and resolutely abandon all he possesses, in order to cleave unto Him,
may He be blessed, and to be absorbed in His light with an attachment
and longing. (Tanya I, p. 316)

Another kind of meditative technique consists of developing a present centered consciousness whereby one is conscious of each action,
and attention is paid to whatever one is doing at the moment. In
Jewish mysticism, high value is placed on a meditative prescription
called "kavanah," or intention. Kavanah denotes concentration and
devotion in whatever one is doing, so that the activity serves as a
means of union with God. A hasidic anecdote illustrates this idea:

A hasid asked his Rebbe: "How can I best serve God?" expecting to hear a
profound and esoteric answer. The Rebbe replied: "One can serve God best with
whatever one is doing at the moment."

The principle of "In all your ways know Him" (Proverbs, 3:6) reflects
this same idea, as the Hebrew word for "knowledge" connotes union, as
in "And Adam knew Eve" (Genesis, 4:1).

Kavanah can be seen as a powerful technique for opening up a mode
of awareness by breaking down habitual, unconscious ways of responding, leading to greater awareness of the details which comprise reality.
Regardless of one's activities, kavanah leads to attachment or union
with God, through concentration on the religious act:

For this should be his kavanah when occupying himself with the Torah
or the particular commandment, that his Divine soul as well as his vital
soul, together with their "garments," shall cleave to Him. (Tanya I, pp.
258–259)

In fact, the term "mitzvah" (commandment) denotes attachment (tzavtah) to God. The same holds true for prayer, the underlying meaning of which is

> to attach oneself to God—not a petition or request, since even those who do not need anything are required to pray. (Likutei Sichos 2, p. 410)

VI

Conventional consciousness sees what is "out there" through the screen of desires, needs, fears, etc. This ego-centered awareness is actually seen as a distorted consciousness. Hasidic teachings focus particularly on overcoming this constricted, ego-centered consciousness, and emphasize the development of "bittul hayesh," a state of egolessness, resulting in an expansive state. In the words of R. Schneur Zalman of Liadi, the founder of the Chabad school:

> When one goes forth from one's own ego, the human, physical "I," through the service of prayer and attachment to Divinity, then one sees the Divine Light. (Sepher Hasichos, p. 126)

The limitations of ego-centered consciousness, what hasidic thought calls the bounds of the "animal soul," must be transcended so as to realize the "Divine soul." Liberation from ego-centered consciousness is referred to as redemption, or a spiritual exodus from Egypt. This redemption, or exodus, is to be experienced daily in one's spiritual growth.

The Bible stipulates that one must remember daily the exodus from Egypt (*Deuteronomy*, 16:3), and the Talmud declares "A person is obligated to view oneself as if having left Egypt that very day" (Talmud, *Pesahim*, 116b). This exodus refers to overcoming the constrictions of ego-centered consciousness.

> In truth, the whole Torah speaks about redemption, since there is no free man except he who is engaged in Torah. Through Torah the soul achieves freedom from the exile of the body and animal soul. (Likutei Sichos 2, p. 371)

The development of an expanded consciousness through destructuring ego-centered consciousness by prayer and Divine service does not mean that one is to forsake the world for selfish spiritual growth.

The central purpose is to bring the realization of the unity of God in the world by transforming it into an abode for His dwelling. However, to do this, one must remain separated from the world; to be in the world but not of it. (Likutei Sichos 3, p. 794)

> Chassidus . . . sees the Jew's central purpose as the unifying link between the Creator and Creation. (The Jew's) purpose is to realize the transcendency and unity of his nature, and of the world in which he lives, within the absolute unity of God. (Tanya I, preface)

Such practices as ecstatic body swaying during prayer, emotional praying, fasting, drinking during a farbrengen (celebration), dancing and singing all facilitate the destructuring of ego-centered consciousness through breaking out of one's self limitations. It is only in non-ordinary states of consciousness that one can acheve control over the autonomic nervous system (Weil, 1972). Thus, hasidic stories abound with tales of wonderworking zaddikim who transcended the conventional laws of physical reality.

VI

One major difference between the Jewish mystical tradition and the esoteric psychologies is that the former, although often addressing itself to right hemisphere, receptive mode consciousness, is always tied to the left hemispheric consciousness of normative Judaism (the revealed as opposed to hidden Torah). As a result Jewish mysticism can be an intellectual study as well as an experiential process. Indeed, the synthesis and harmony between the "rational" and "non-rational," the awareness of the mystical in the rational and the rational in the mystical, unites the workings of the two hemispheres into an integrated consciousness. Straitjacketing Judaism in the rational framework exclusively, or developing an antinomian Jewish mysticism, distorts Judaism and truncates consciousness. Jewish mystical teaching does, however, share with the esoteric psychologies a concern with the extended consciousness, which it links to ultimate reality and which is given immediate expression through the religious context.

References

Assagioli, R. *The act of will*. New York: Viking Press, 1973.
Blackburn, T. R. Sensuous-intellectual complementarity in science. In R. Ornstein (Ed.), *The nature of human consciousness*. New York: Viking Press, 1974.
Bogen, J. E. The other side of the brain: An appositional mind. In R. Ornstein (Ed.), *The nature of human consciousness*. New York: Viking Press, 1974.
Castenada, C. *The teachings of Don Juan: A yaqui way of knowledge*. Berkeley: University of California Press, 1968.

Castenada, C. *Journey to Ixtlan: The lessons of Don Juan.* New York: Simon and Schuster, 1972.

Castenada, C. *A separate reality: Conversations with Don Juan.* New York: Simon and Schuster, 1971.

Deikman, A. J. Bimodal consciousness. In R. Ornstein (Ed.), *The nature of human consciousness.* New York: Viking Press, 1974.

Gazzaniga, M. S. The split brain in man. In R. Ornstein (Ed.), *The nature of human consciousness.* New York: Viking Press, 1974.

Hebb, D. O. Science and the world of imagination. *Canadian Journal of Psychology,* 1975, *1,* 4–11.

The Holy Scriptures (2 vols.). Philadelphia: Jewish Publication Society, 1917.

Lee, D. L. Codifications of reality: Lineal and non-lineal. In R. Ornstein (Ed.), *The nature of human consciousness.* New York: Viking Press, 1974.

LeShan, L. *The medium, the mystic, and the physicist: Toward a general theory of the paranormal.* New York: Viking Press, 1974.

Likutei Sichos (4 vols.). Brooklyn, New York: Kehot Publication Society, 1964.

Ornstein, R. *The psychology of consciousness.* New York: Viking Press, 1972.

Pearce, J. C. *The crack in the cosmic egg.* New York: Julian Press, 1975.(a)

Pearce, J. C. *Exploring the crack in the cosmic egg.* New York: Julian Press, 1975.(b)

Roszak, T. *The making of a counter culture.* New York: Doubleday, 1969.

Schneur Zalman of Liadi. Tanya (vol. 1) (N. Mindel, trans.). Brooklyn, New York: Kehot Publication Society, 1965.

Sepher Hasichos 5701. Brooklyn, New York: Kehot Publication Society, 1964.

Sperry, R. W. Neurology and the mind brain problem. In R. Isaacson (Ed.), *Basic readings in neuropsychology.* New York: Harper and Row, 1964.

The Talmud (18 vols.). I. Epstein (Ed.). London: Soncino Press, 1961.

Tart, C. T. *States of consciousness.* New York: Dutton, 1975.

Weil, A. *The natural mind: A new way of looking at drugs and the higher consciousness.* Boston: Houghton Mifflin, 1972.

The Zohar (5 vols.). H. Sperling and M. Simon (Trans.). London: Soncino Press, 1934.

Precognition and the Prophetic Tradition: From ESP to the Effective Myth

Jan Ehrenwald

Precognition is one of the most puzzling modalities of the psi syndrome studied by modern parapsychologists. The other modalities are ESP or direct mind-to-mind communication; clairvoyance or direct extrasensory perception of external objects and configurations; and psychokinesis (PK), or direct impact of volition on external material targets. This is popularly described as "mind over matter." It was the apparent absurdity of such modalities that prompted J.B. Rhine and his associates (1947) to develop a variety of laboratory tests for their methodical investigation. The ensuing controversy is a matter of historical record. Despite last ditch efforts to discredit the mass of statistical evidence that has accumulated during the past four decades, there is now growing consensus about the validity of experimental results. The probability against chance of the Soal-Goldney (1954) or the more recent Helmut Schmidt (1974) experiments with playing cards or with a more sophisticated automated scoring device using the decay of a radio-active element as a randomizing principle, amounts to truly astronomical figures. They indicate that some persons are indeed capable of "guessing" correctly specific ESP targets *ahead* of time, even though the correct hits occur in a haphazard, random manner, with a precognitive time span amounting to seconds or fractions of seconds.

Although the factual evidence, especially of the more recent automated tests, can no longer be doubted, their interpretation is still problematical. Informed critics as well as parapsychologists themselves have raised the question whether or not it would be more parsimonious to explain precognition in terms of "mere" psychokinesis, a "mind over matter" effect, emanating from the subject or experimenter, rather than in terms of a truly mindblowing reversal of the causal chain— that is, in terms of an "effect" preceding its "cause".

II

The question of true precognition versus PK is still *sub judice*. It is reminiscent of the Heisenberg effect in quantum mechanics, according to which the observer has a hand in affecting the status of the target of observations on the subatomic, microphysical level. But even so, there can be little doubt that precognition or its purported PK equivalent confronts us with an apparent break in the ironclad laws of cause and effect, of the irreversibility of pre-Einsteinian time, with the whole gamut of its attendant temporo-spatial anomalies. It is virtually incompatible with traditional habits of thinking in the Western world, with Kant's *a priori* categories of space, time and causality, or with what the Cambridge philosopher C.D. Broad has described as the "limiting principles" of science.

But informed critics have also been puzzled by the patently trivial, meaningless nature of precognition incidents of this order. I pointed out elsewhere (1967, 1975) that apparent precognition under laboratory conditions is wholly disparate from and incommensurable with precognitive utterances of a higher order in which a seer, a prophet, a holy man, seems capable of catching veridical glimpses of things to come, foretelling future events that affect the lives of individuals and the destinies of nations, if not humankind as a whole.

As a matter of basic principle, incidents of the card-calling, laboratory type, are essentially flaw-determined. They are due to random fluctuations or minor imperfections in the protective screen of the central nervous system designed to ward off the intrusion of biologically irrelevant outside stimuli into conscious awareness. Stimuli that happen to pass the filter are, in effect, laboratory artifacts that would otherwise remain unnoticed.

Trivial extrasensory impressions of this type have to be contrasted with what I describe as need-determined psi incidents; that is, with the occasional perception and central processing of telepathic, clairvoyant or precognitive stimuli of a higher order that are capable, on rare but psychodynamically well-defined occasions, to break through the screen and make their appearance in conscious awareness. It is known today that they do so in answer to powerful motivations, to the pressing needs of those involved in the incidents. They can be described as need-determined.

III

Divination, prophecy, premonitory dreams and related veridical experiences are classical examples of such need-determined manifestations of the psi syndrome. It is true that they usually lack the evidential value possessed by statistical mass experiments of the card-calling type. They cannot be validated by reference to "points of significance," "critical ratios" or chi-squares. They have to rely on human testimony, documentary evidence and related source materials upon which the historic method is based. But they can be supported by extrapolation from the concerted evidence of well-authenticated laboratory findings which indicate that psi phenomena in general, and precognitive responses in particular, do in reality occur—irrespective of the formidable odds that have piled against them.

Despite the differences, there is a unifying bond between the minor and major classes of psi phenomena. Both are dramatic illustrations of the vast scope and indeed unlimited potential of the human mind.

Nevertheless, shifting the focus from prediction to prophecy makes necessary what can be described as a veritable existential shift. One has to make a quantum jump from the scientific to a transcendental, if not supernatural order of things; from the measurable and quantifiable, to what is immeasurable and ineffable; from the personal to the transpersonal; from the profane to the numinous and the sublime.

The ancient Greek concept of divination and soothsaying, as exemplified by the figures of Calchas, Mopsus or Tiresias, are somewhere between the two categories. According to Homer, Calchas was the wisest of them all, and knew everything that had been, now is, or would be in the future. Yet when Calchas challenged the soothsayer Mopsus to tell him the number of figs growing on a tree nearby, it turned out that Mopsus "out-guessed" Calchas. In the ensuing competition between the two, Calchas lost out once more and died from a broken heart. It will be noted that Mopsus' feat of hitting a bulls-eye on his arboreal target is closely reminiscent of the exploits of modern parapsychological percipients. So is the oft quoted boast of the Delphic Oracle that it can "count the sands and measure the Ocean". Yet it was followed by a fairly correct account of the menu King Croesus was having at a barbecue hundreds of miles away. There are scores of similar narratives in ancient Greco-Roman literature. Some of them, like Cassandra foretelling the Fall of Troy, or the Delphic Oracle presaging the misfortune that was to befall the House of Thebes, pertain to historic or mythological events of a much higher order. They are, in effect, close to more meaningful, "need-determined" versions of psi.

Nevertheless, they still lack three basic features that are characteristic of the prophetic tradition: they fail to draw a sharp line of demarcation between good and evil; they are uncommitted to higher moral principles; nor are they the ecstatic utterances of passionate religious reformers or charismatic leaders. With rare exceptions, ethically committed prophecies of this order are the principle domain of the Biblical tradition. The classical prototype is, of course, Isaiah. Isaiah "predicted" that Assyria would be the instrument through which punishment would be visited on the children of Israel to purge them of their sins. But by contrast to Cassandra, he foretold "merited" disaster.

Yet, by the same token, Cecil Roth (1965) emphasizes that Isaiah's prophecies also had a comforting side, in that the triumph of a foreign power was not to be final. Together with denunciations of moral shortcomings, Isaiah drew the picture of brighter, Messianic days to come. In a similar vein, Jeremiah, the prophet of doom, made his prophecies expressly conditional. ". . . Amend your ways and your doings and I will cause you to dwell in this place" (*Jeremiah* 7:3). And he quoted God's explicit command: ". . . Hearken unto my voice, and I will be your God, and ye shall be My people . . ." (*Jeremiah* 7:23).

Such dramatic utterances throw into sharp relief the contrast between the activistic commitment of Jewish prophetic tradition and the Greco-Roman fatalistic acquiescence with a pre-ordained inexorable destiny. Viewed against the religious fervor of the great prophets of Biblical times, the showmanship of the Greek soothsayers and the cryptic ambiguity of the oracles pale into insignificance. Eliahu Auerbach (1966) stresses that the lighthearted and bantering tone with which Homer described the weaknesses of the Greek gods was entirely foreign to the spirit of Israel as expressed in prophecy. The prophets did not "precognize". They foretold events in a conditional way, and they were in deadly earnest about what they had to say.

IV

There undoubtedly is a far cry from the parapsychologist's laboratory to the process of "experimental" history-in-the-making in either
modern or Biblical times. But both have one thing in common: the chief
protagonist in both the laboratory, and on the stage of history, is the
person with a mission, propelled by high hopes, wishes and
motivations. They range from the trivial—if not the ridiculous—to the
sublime and numinous in the historic, if not cosmic perspective.

There is yet another common denominator between precognition in
the laboratory, and the proving ground of experimental history—
provided that such a thing in reality exists. In both instances, one's
motivations, hopes and expectations are bound to have *consequences*. I
noted that the experimenter in the parapsychological lab—not unlike
Heisenberg's observer of microphysical, quantum mechanical events
on the subatomic plane—is apt to influence the behavior of the target
of observations. It is true, Helmut Schmidt, the parapsychologist, was
not quite sure whether or not he himself had affected the results reg-
istered by his precognitive automatic scoring device. But to the extent
to which he did just that, his experiment in precognition was, in effect,
an example of telepathic or psychokinetic self-fulfillment. He brought
about the event which he tried to predict.

The reader willing to join in yet another exercise of the existential
shift, will perhaps note at this point that from here to what theologians
have described as the *effective*—and in effect *self-fulfilling*—myth is
only one, though admittedly mind boggling step. The fact is that
Isaiah's or Jeremiah's predictions ". . . that the mountain of the Lord's
house shall be established as the top of the mountains . . ." (*Isaiah* 2:2);
that "out of Zion shall go forth the law . . ." (*Isaiah* 2:3); and that ". . . I
will cause you to dwell in this place" (*Jeremiah* 7:3) have indeed come
close to self-fulfillment. Seen in this light, they have turned out to be
supremely successful experiments on a vast historical scale.

The question is, whether self-fulfilling prophecies or myths have
anything to do with psi phenomena, or with what J.B. Rhine has called
experimental religion. It was hinted earlier that clear-cut quantifiable
answers can only be elicited in response to clear-cut quantifiable questions. Such a well-rehearsed question-and-answer game is clearly in-
applicable to the Biblical or, for that matter, to the ancient Greco-
Roman or Far-Eastern religious tradition. But in the last analysis, the
similarity between a high ESP score in the laboratory and an effective
myth in a religious setting is unmistakable. It is evidently due to the
origin of both "effects" from the same trans-personal symbiotic matrix

from which both trivial and numinous psi experiences emerge. Both are predicated on the hopes and motivations—or, on a more exalted plane—on the chiliastic expectations and the personal charisma of the "experimenters" who carry the seeds of their telepathic self-fulfillment within themselves.

Still, the similarity of a burst of extra-chance scoring by a gifted psychic and the ecstatic utterances of a prophet stops at this point. The realms of the sacred and numinous still maintain their extraterritorial status inaccessible to sober scientific exploration. Rhine's proposed experimental religion is likely to be nothing but a pious wish of the father of parapsychology, and the chasm separating the two domains remains as deep as that between a card-calling test and a theophany, or between a Bunsen burner in the laboratory and the Burning Bush in the Sinai Desert. Both are predicated on a breakthrough from the natural order of things to a world transcending the natural order. It is a breakthrough which is beyond the dreams of the philosophers or social scientists of a past generation. Apparently, religion and its ultimate concerns are still bound to remain the preserves of the theologian and the plain religious believer.

References

Auerbach, E. The prophets. In D. Ben Gurion (Ed.). *The Jews in their land.* New York: Doubleday, 1966.

Ehrenwald, J. Precognition, prophecy and self-fulfillment in greco-roman, hebrew and aztec antiquity. *International Journal of Parapsychology,* 1967, 9(4), 227–233.

Ehrenwald, J. Cerebral localization and the psi syndrome. *Journal of nervous and mental disease,* 1975, 161(6), 393–398.

The Holy Scriptures (2 vols.). Philadelphia: Jewish Publication Society, 1917.

Rhine, J.B. *The reach of the mind.* New York: Sloan Associates, 1947.

Roth, C. *History of the jews.* New York: Schocken Books, 1965.

Schmidt, H. Instrumentation in the parapsychological laboratory. In J. Beloff (Ed.). *New directions in parapsychology.* London: Elec Science, 1974.

Soal, S. F. & Bateman, F. *Modern experiments in telepathy.* New Haven: Yale University Press, 1954.

Hasidism and Logotherapy:
Encounter Through Anthology

Reuven P. Bulka

In the experience of Viktor Frankl, architect of logotherapy, reactions to his lectures seem to vary with the place where the lecture is given. Generally, when Frankl travels east, what he says is not greeted with as much enthusiasm as when he speaks in the western world. The eastern world seems to think of logotherapy as something which they knew all along. In the west, logotherapy seems to be something novel.

Frankl has never claimed that his system is, in fact, something new under the sun. He takes the approach that one must rediscover the basic truths of human existence. Logotherapy, in fact, is geared towards facilitating this discovery. It, therefore, would seem quite pertinent to illustrate the similarity logotherapy shares with eastern tradition by comparing logotherapy with some basic notions of Hasidism, the movement launched by Rabbi Israel Baal Shem Tov in the middle of the 18th century. In fact, Hasidism is rooted in Jewish mystical tradition and has branched forth with many different "schools" headed by leaders called *rebbes* and peopled with varying numbers of disciples.

Instead of taking any specific doctrine, this article focuses on incidents and statements associated with many of the hasidic rabbis and
offers a logotherapeutic counterpart to each incident or observation.

The hasidic incidents referred to in this paper are mainly those
which may be found in *The Hasidic Anthology* (Newman, 1963). This is
used as it contains a broad base of subject topics which incorporate the
ideas of many of the hasidic masters and is also an easily accessible
volume.

The logotherapeutic counterparts herein projected are mainly not
direct quotes of Frankl but rather the paraphrasing of ideas either
directly expressed by Frankl or graphically implied in the system
Frankl develops.

The Notion of Free-Will in Hasidism and Logotherapy

Hasidism—The Koretzer Rebbe reflected on the fact that if one's desires are weakened as the body declines, what happens to free will?
Contrary to the argument that such an individual might sin less because there is a weaker impulse to sin, the Koretzer maintained that
the impulse, though it may be weaker because the body is weakening,
is nevertheless strong by force of habit. Besides, the power of resistance
is commensurately weakened.

Logotherapy—The individual in all situations and all circumstances
always retains the free will to take a stand towards those circumstances.

Hasidism—According to Rabbi Israel Baal Shem Tov, one should learn
pride but not be proud, one should learn anger but not feel angry, for
the person should be complete, possessing all human traits. The
Koretzer observed that one cannot be consciously good unless one
knows evil. One cannot appreciate pleasure unless one has experienced
bitterness. Good is merely the opposite of evil, as is pleasure the opposite of anxiety. Without the evil impulse one could do no evil but
neither could one do good.

Logotherapy—It is preferable to have a world in which even Hitler is
possible rather than one in which all individuals are programmed.
Such programming destroys the element of choice and makes of any
good behavior an action devoid of the human ingredient and therefore,
lacking meaning. It is only because of the possibility of evil that choice
is possible.

Hasidism—The Dzikover Rebbe stopped an individual and asked what he would do if he found a purse of money. The fellow replied instantly—I would return it to the owner, of course. The rabbi said he had too quick an answer and that it was probably insincere. Another responded that he would probably keep it if he could. The rabbi said that he was wicked. The Dzikover then approached an unlearned hasid who responded—Rabbi, it would be such a great temptation. I would beg God to give me the strength to withstand it and thus enable me to perform the commandment of returning a lost article. The rabbi acknowledged that this answer was proper and correct. He further said that it was proper for a hasid to give such an answer. Opponents of Hasidism blame us for accepting unlearned persons as hasidim, he said, but this shows the influence of hasidic instruction even among the unlearned.

Logotherapy—It is quite useful to learn from the wisdom of the man in the street. Sometimes there is a tension in human action which involves doing what one ought to do as opposed to what one would like to do. It might be pertinent here to relate a story told by Frankl (1966) of a Jewish army doctor who, during World War I, hid in the ditches together with his dear friend, a high ranking aristocrat who was also a colonel, while the heavy bombing of the Italian/Austrian border started. The colonel teased his friend saying, "Dr. Rosenbloom, we are watching the inferiority of the semitic race because now you certainly feel anguish, don't you?" Dr. Rosenbloom replied calmly: "dear colonel, of course I admit I do feel anguish but why invoke the inferiority of one race and the superiority of the other? If you felt as much anguish as I now do you might have long ago run away." What matters, Frankl adds, is not the emotions we have but the attitude we take towards them. What matters is not whether we would want to take the money purse, but whether we could overcome the strong desire to take it.

The Nature of Human Striving in Hasidism and Logotherapy

Hasidism—After Rabbi Uri Strelisker died, one of his disciples came to Rabbi Bunam who asked what specific character trait Rabbi Uri desired to instill in his hasidim. The hasid thought that Rabbi Uri desired to make his hasidim very humble. The rabbi would order a rich hasid to draw water at the pump and to bring in the pail on his shoulder, something the man would never have done at home. Rabbi Bunam said that he works differently. He explained with a parable. Three men convicted of a crime were locked in a dark cell. Two were intelligent, the third witless. When food was lowered to them, the witless person did not know how to take his share and would either break the plate or cut himself. One of the other prisoners tried to help him by rehearsing the necessary behavior, but the next day, a different food arrangement would be sent and the witless one would be perplexed. The third prisoner then remarked, "Why do you waste time teaching the fellow every day? Let me bore a hole into the wall to admit some light and then he will be able to help himself." Continued Rabbi Bunam, "I try to admit into the human soul the awe and love of God. This is the light from which one can learn wise behavior in its totality and not trait by trait."

Logotherapy—There are different layers and dimensions to the human being but the spiritual dimension, which is the uniquely human one, is the higher dimension in that it includes the somatic and the psychic.

Hasidism—Rabbi Menachem Mendel of Vitebsk said that before the endlessness of God, the highest saint and the lowliest commoner are equal.

Logotherapy—The corollary to monotheism is "monanthropism"— that is, the notion of the oneness of God may be paralleled by the notion of the oneness of humankind, all equal in their potential for good.

Hasidism—According to the Medzibozer, the individual has been placed in the world to contribute towards the improvement of the world. The hermit who avoids the society of people is inclined towards wickedness.

Logotherapy—The purpose of life is not achieved through self-actualization or self-realization, but rather through self-transcendence and orientation around "causes greater than oneself, and persons other than oneself."

Hasidism—The Kossover said that if one gives a donation to a poor person who then returns the donation asking for an even larger gift, agreement to this request brings boundless reward since such reaction is contrary to human nature.

Logotherapy—The key element in the human dynamics, along with self- transcendence, is "self-detachment;" that is, rising above oneself, thus becoming capable of judging oneself, and, if need be, opposing oneself.

Hasidism—According to the Kotzker every commandment should be performed with the proper intention, with one exception—humility.

Logotherapy—Certain actions of the individual demand the exercise of will. There are others which can only be realized in spontaneity if they are to be authentic. They cannot focus on the self for then such actions are stripped of their meaning. To be humble means, in a sense, to be oblivious of the self so that intending to be humble paradoxically makes humility impossible. Frankl also invokes the example of good conscience: fulfill your responsibilities, and good conscience will accrue; strive for good conscience, and it will elude you, because there is no ground for good conscience unless you have met your responsibilities.

Hasidism—Rabbi Bunam said—One should be careful of every move one makes in life just like the chess player is careful before making a move. Before any action is taken, one should anticipate whether there will be cause to regret the move.

Logotherapy—The leading maxim of existential analysis exhorts people to imagine that they are living now for the second time and had acted as wrongly the first time as they are about to act now.

Hasidism—The Lubliner said that he loves more a wicked person who is aware of this wickedness than he loves a good person who is aware of personal goodness.

Logotherapy—Life is a continual striving process towards reaching values. One must continually be aware of one's finiteness and the fact that there is so much more to achieve. Being always lags behind meaning: "meaning must be ahead of being. Meaning sets the pace for being" (Frankl, 1968, p. 12).

Hasidism—The Lizensker Rebbe said that only God is perfect. Human actions must basically be partially defective. If one believes that one's good deed or holy study is thoroughly pure and perfect, then it is a sign that the individual is thoroughly bad.

Logotherapy—Only to the extent that man acknowledges his finiteness is he able to overcome it.

Hasidism—The Lubliner Rebbe was once asked why he took snuff in the midst of prayers even though interruptions were forbidden. The Lubliner in response told the story of a king who heard a street singer playing the violin. He liked the player and invited him to the king's court. The violinist would frequently break his routine because of a broken string. A member of the court finally asked the singer why he did not just restring his instrument to avoid interruptions. The street singer replied that obviously the king had many musicians with perfect instruments whom he could easily order to sing for him, but he prefers to hear me, which would indicate that he wants to hear my imperfect violin. Likewise, continued the Lubliner, God has an abundance of singing angels yet He has commanded that we pray to Him, so it is therefore clear that God is willing to tolerate our weaknesses.

Logotherapy—If all human beings were perfect then every human being would be the same and thus all human beings would be replaceable. There would be no individual uniqueness. It is precisely the imperfections within each individual which make for the differences and thus for the unique quality of every human being.

Hasidism—The Kaminker Rebbe tells that he once resolved to devote a whole day to the recitation of Psalms. Towards evening he was finishing when he was told that his rabbi, the Tzidnover Maggid, wanted to see him. The Kaminker said he would come as soon as he was finished but the Maggid told his messenger to insist that he come immediately. The Maggid asked the Kaminker why he did not come at first and the Kaminker told him the reason. The Maggid responded that he had called the Kaminker to make a collection for a poor Jew. Psalms can be sung by angels but only mortals can help the poor. Charity is greater than reciting the Psalms since angels cannot perform charity.

Logotherapy—The nature of meaning resides in the uniqueness of the individual, where the individual is irreplaceable, plus the uniqueness of the moment, which is irrepeatable. What others can do as well cannot signify a personal meaning, nor would it be meaningful to use the moment if we were immortal, and thus could postpone everything.

Value-Orientation in Hasidism and Logotherapy

Hasidism—Rabbi Leib Saras questions the value of someone who studies Torah (Jewish law), but who nevertheless is full of pride and temper. Rather the person should be the Torah itself and other individuals should be able to learn how to behave from observing such an individual's conduct.

Logotherapy—Values cannot be taught. They must be lived.

Hasidism—According to the Kotzker Rebbe, there are three characters in the person about to perform a good deed. The one who says, "I shall do it soon" is a poor character; the one who says, "I am ready to do it now" is of average quality; and the one who says, "I am doing it" is praiseworthy.

Logotherapy—Life is a task. The nature of the human task is not one which is realized through reflection, but through action. The human being is called upon to respond to the meaning offered by each life situation, and to actualize the meaning potential of the moment. The moment which has been wasted through failure to actualize meaning has been irrecoverably lost.

Hasidism—According to the "Yud" there are three character types among those who serve God—the one who labors all day but believes that nothing has been accomplished is at the highest point of merit; one who has done nothing to serve God and is aware of this is of average merit; one who is righteous and proud of this is least commendable. Such a person indulges in self deception and devotion to Torah and the commandments is wasted.

Logotherapy—A basic element of the human endeavor is the awareness of the infinite value possibility. One must constantly be aware that values are waiting to be actualized and that no matter how much has been achieved, there is always so much more left. One who fails to recognize this stagnates.

Hasidism—The "Yud" observed that one who does not feel one has improved in holiness during the day certainly has fallen back and was better the day before. The person always moves and never stands still. If one does not advance, one falls back.

Logotherapy—One must be aware of the value possibilities constantly confronting the individual and behave responsibly towards this awareness. There is a subject/object tension within which the human being oscillates. One is constantly challenged to transcend the real state toward the ideal one. Failure to indulge in this dynamic essentially removes the individual from the human dimension and is thus a regression.

Hasidism—The Gerer Rebbe once asked a young man if he had learned Torah. "Just a little," responded the man, to which the Gerer retorted, "That is all that anyone has ever learned of the Torah."

Logotherapy—Life offers infinite possibilities. The individual is finite and therefore can never exhaust the infinite possibilities. But the individual must try: "Things are bad," Frankl says. "But unless we do our best to improve them, everything will become worse" (1975, p. 84).

Hasidism—The Sassover Rebbe used to go to county fairs and help people in need. On one occasion, some cattlemen left their animals standing in the marketplace, exceedingly thirsty, whilst they went to attend to their affairs. When the Sassover Rebbe saw this, he brought a bucket and gave the calves to drink. One dealer who came back from an errand and saw this mistook the Sassover for a hired hand and commanded the Sassover to give water to his cattle. The Sassover gladly obeyed and after he gave the animals to drink was given a coin by the dealer. He refused to accept it, saying, "Go away, I did not feed the cattle because you ordered me but because God ordered me, God who commands us to be merciful to God's creatures."

Logotherapy—Do not do things for thereby gaining power or pleasure. Do things for their own sake, or for the sake of another person.

The Element of Meaning in Hasidism and Logotherapy

Hasidism—A young man came to the Riziner Rebbe wanting to receive rabbinical ordination. The Riziner asked the fellow about his daily conduct. The young man said that he always dressed in white, drank only water, placed tacks in his shoes for self-mortification, rolled naked in the snow and ordered the synagogue caretaker to give him forty stripes daily on his bare back. Just at that moment, a white horse entered the Rebbe's courtyard, drank water, and began rolling in the snow. "See," said the Rebbe to the young man, "this creature is white, drinks only water, has nails in its shoes, rolls in the snow and surely gets more than forty stripes a day, yet is nothing but a horse."

Logotherapy—It is not the act itself which is crucial. It is the meaning with which the act is invested, the human quality, which gives it value.

Hasidism—The Baal Shem Tov recommended that it is desirable for a person to frequently interrupt one's occupation for a short pause and concentrate upon the awe of God, even if involved in a sacred occupation.

Logotherapy—The individual should not act along the lines of rote mechanistic behavior but rather orient around meaning and purpose, even in endeavors which on their own may be meaningful. Approaching them mechanistically eliminates the meaning perspective. The awareness of why one performs an action greatly affects the how.

Hasidism—Rabbi Leib Saras said that he did not journey to Rabbi Dov Baer of Mezeritz to learn interpretations of the Torah, but rather to study how Rabbi Dov Baer tied his shoelaces and took off his shoes. What worth are the meanings given to the Torah? It is in one's actions, one's speech, one's bearing and loyalty to God that one makes manifest the Torah.

Logotherapy—This is a "man in the street" type of orientation which emphasizes that it is not the ivory tower dialectic which is crucial but the daily lifestyle which is lived meaningfully by virtue of the "pre-reflective ontological self-understanding;" by which term Frankl ultimately means the "wisdom of the heart" (1975, p. 124).

Hasidism—A person once approached the Kotzker Rebbe asking that the rabbi pray that the individual's sons would study the Torah diligently. The Kotzker replied, "If your sons will see that you are a diligent student, they will follow your example. However, if you neglect your own studies and just wish that your sons study, they will do just as you do when they grow up. They will neglect Torah study but will want that their sons study."

Logotherapy—Meaning can never be pushed off into the next generation. What is meaningless in itself does not become meaningful by extending its existence over generations. To think that by having children one has found true meaning would be to push off meaning into the next generation, but each generation would then do this ad infinitum. Instead, meaning must be found in the here and now and children then will carry that meaning into future generations. Frankl himself tells the story of a man who bought a parrot and tried to get the parrot to call him "Daddy," but the parrot did not cooperate. The owner, in frustration, punished the uncooperative parrot by locking it overnight in a hen house. In the morning, when he came to take the parrot from its prison, all but one of the chickens had been killed by the parrot. The parrot was holding the lone surviving chicken in its claws and shouting incessantly, "Call me Daddy! Call me Daddy! Call me Daddy!" The parrot behaved in as authoritarian a manner as its owner, and, like the owner, received no cooperation from those of whom the demands were made.

Hasidism—The Porissover Rebbe said that if a person is poor and meek, it is easy for that individual to be joyful as that individual has nothing to be afraid of losing.

Logotherapy—One can overcome fear by confronting fear-arousing situations, even "paradoxically" wishing to happen what one had been afraid of all along.

Attitudes to Despair, Suffering, and Death in Hasidism and Logotherapy

Hasidism—The Kobriner Rebbe tells that when he was a young boy there was a famine in which the poor went from village to village begging for food. Some came to his mother's house and she began to bake for them. Some of the poor beggars became impatient and started insulting the rabbi's mother who began to cry. Still a boy, the future Kobriner Rebbe said to his mother, "Why should you be bothered by their insults?

In fact, their insults make it possible for you to help them with a pure heart and to do a good deed in perfect spirit. If they had praised you, you might have done the good deed in order to gain their praises and this would have made your deed less praiseworthy than now when you are doing it entirely in fulfillment of God's command and for the sake of serving God."

Logotherapy—The individual, in all situations, even in situations of despair, can ovecome the despair through taking the proper attitude to the situation, thereby finding a meaning to the very despair.

Hasidism—The Lubliner Rebbe commented that God becomes attentive to the person who sings in the midst of personal troubles and accepts these troubles good-naturedly and with laughter.

Logotherapy—Adverse circumstances are not meaningless but offer the possibility to fulfill even the deepest possible meaning; that is, "to turn tragedy into a personal triumph, to turn one's predicament into a human achievement" (Frankl, 1977).

Hasidism—Rabbi Isaac Meyer of Ger had thirteen sons, all of whom died. At the death of the youngest, it was impossible to comfort his wife. Rabbi Isaac Meyer said to her, "Our sons have not died in vain. If a misfortune such as this should befall others, they will remember that Isaac Meyer lost thirteen holy sons and so they will not feel angry against God."

Logotherapy—The meaning of life is unconditional, even in cases of intense suffering. There is a meaning to life in the suffering which makes the suffering bearable. Despair associated with suffering exists only because one fails to see a meaning in the suffering itself.

Hasidism—When Rabbi Bunam was lying on his death bed, his wife cried bitter tears. He said to her, "Why do you cry? All my life has been given to me merely so that I should learn how to die."

Logotherapy—Without death, human life cannot be complete. And death is another challenge to take a proper attitude, and, by so doing, "rise above, and grow beyond oneself" (Frankl, 1977). A good death is the culmination of a good life.

Hasidism—The Gerer asked why a person fears dying. Is not death a return to God in Heaven? The reason for the fear is that in the future world, one gains a clear perspective of all one's deeds on earth. The individual who becomes aware of the senseless things committed on earth cannot abide the self and in that awareness inheres Hell.

Logotherapy—It is only the individual who has not lived properly who is afraid to die. If life is a "becoming" process then in death one has attained "being" (Frankl, 1978, p. 112). If one has lived a complete life then death as a natural culmination of life is easier to accept.

Hasidism—The Belzer Rebbe heard a man express a wish to die like a good Jew. The Belzer retorted, "You should rather desire to live like a good Jew and it will follow in consequence that you will die a good Jew."

Logotherapy—"Man's past is his true future" (Frankl, 1978, p. 112). What has been achieved can never be erased.

A Comparison of the Nature of Love in Hasidism and Logotherapy

Hasidism—Rabbi Shlomo Karliner said that God treats a person in the same way that one treats one's children. If you do not neglect your children, God will not neglect you.

Logotherapy—Love is not something which can be demanded. The individual lives out humanness best by transcending the self, by immersing the self in the other. The individual thereby generates a pattern of concern for the other which, in turn, brings out the best in the couple.

Hasidism—Rabbi Moshe Leib of Sassov said that to truly love means to know what brings pain to your friend.

Logotherapy—True love involves self-transcendence towards the "thou" and to be concerned about the other. The true fulfillment of the self comes via fulfilling the other individual.

Hasidism—Moshe Leib Sassover sat at the bedside of the sick in his city, nursing and caring for them. He said that one who cannot suck the matter from the boils of a child stricken with the plague has not reached to one half the ultimate level of love for one's fellow beings.

Logotherapy—True love involves "forgetting oneself by giving oneself" (Frankl, 1977).

Hasidism—The Berditschever said that one who serves God out of fear never forgets one's own existence but still fears God, but the one who serves out of love forgets about the self entirely.

Logotherapy—In true love, one does not focus on the self, but one is immersed in the other.

Perspectives on Work and Material Gain in Hasidism and Logotherapy

Hasidism—According to the Kotzker, the prohibition against making idols includes the prohibition against making idols out of the commandments. One should not think that the purpose of a commandment resides in the outer form and that the inner meaning should not be considered relevant. Instead, the opposite position should be adopted.

Logotherapy—Even in the act of doing that which is very meaningful, such as the practice of medicine, it is not the actual practice which is most meaningful as much as the attitude with which one approaches the profession and the human quality with which one invests the work.

Hasidism—The Baal Shem Tov once went with his son to visit the ailing rabbi of Medziboz. The son was admiring a cabinet full of silverware. The Baal Shem Tov said to his son, "You think in your heart that this silverware is in the wrong place and that it should be in your father's house. You are half right and half wrong. The silverware is in its wrong place, but not because it is not by us. It should rather be given away as charity instead of shining here as futile ornaments."

Logotherapy—The will to meaning is the basic human striving. The will to power confuses the means with the end itself. Power is not an end in itself nor is the acquisition of wealth an end in itself. Instead these are means towards the actualization of values.

Hasidism—Rabbi Nachum Tzernobiler said that if it is a choice between poverty and wealth, he would always choose poverty because poverty is a shield against egotism and any other spiritual evil. It is least costly and most easily obtainable. It doesn't have to struggle with jealousy and competition, it need not respond to questions or suspicions and is understood without comment or explanation. Continues Rabbi Nachum, "I beg of you, my good friends, do not deprive me of this great treasure."

Logotherapy—It is not the circumstance as such which is either meaningful or meaningless, it is rather the approach one takes to that situation. The right attitude can transmute a reality from the suffering dimension into the dimension of meaning.

Hasidism—A hasid once complained to the Kotzker that he was so engrossed in his business that he could not spend time on the study of Talmud and Hasidism. The Kotzker explained to the hasid that God wished to benefit Israel and therefore, gave them many commandments. But, what is the benefit of having the responsibility for many commandments? It is, in fact, a hardship, for it would have been much easier to have just a few precepts which could easily have been observed. The answer is that the variety of precepts allows individuals in different areas to do God's bidding. A farmer, a planter, a house builder, etc., each has specific obligations and therefore can do God's work. The merchant, by being honest, not overcharging and not deceiving, pleases God.

Logotherapy—There is meaning in every situation. The notion of unconditional meaning in life asserts that no situation is devoid of meaning. Even where one is confronted with an unavoidable suffering, one may, through a proper attitude, give that situation its meaning quality.

Conclusion

Hasidism, it will be readily apparent, contains some very profound ideas, but these profound ideas are essentially very simple ideas. They strike at the very core of human existence. The same may be said of the philosophy of logotherapy as well as its clinical approach.

It is not relevant whether the hasidic sages were logotherapists or whether logotherapists are hasidim. The key element is that hasidic sages could easily practice logotherapy and logotherapists could easily be hasidim. Their respective outlooks, attitudes, and approaches are strikingly similar. Moreover, the hasidic masters, unbeknown to them, often practiced what may be termed "meta-clinical therapy," sometimes of a one-to-one nature, sometimes of a group nature. They attempted, by re-orienting distorted thinking, to solve the problems of the masses. That, ironically, is logotherapy's greatest strength.

References

Frankl, V. E. *Three lectures*. Brandeis, California: Brandeis Institute, 1966.
Frankl, V. E. *Psychotherapy and existentialism: Selected papers on logotherapy*. New York: Simon and Schuster, 1968.
Frankl, V. E. *The unconscious god:* Psychotherapy and theology. New York: Simon and Schuster, 1975.
Frankl, V. E. Lecture given at the inauguration of the Frankl Library and Memorabilia. Berkeley, California: Graduate Theological Union, Feb. 12, 1977.
Frankl, V. E. *The unheard cry for meaning: Psychotherapy and humanism*. New York: Simon and Schuster, 1978.
Newman, L. I. *The hasidic anthology: Tales and teachings of the hasidim*. New York: Schocken Books, 1963.

About the Contributors

REUVEN P. BULKA is editor of the *Journal of Psychology and Judaism* and director of the *Centre for the Study of Psychology and Judaism.* He received his Ph.D. from the University of Ottawa in 1971, concentrating on the logotherapy of Viktor Frankl. He maintains a steady contact with Dr. Frankl, and has lectured and written extensively on logotherapy and other topics in various journals, including *Chronical Review, Humanitas, Jewish Digest, Jewish Life, Jewish Spectator,* the *Journal of Ecumenical Studies,* the *Journal of Religion and Health,* and *Tradition.* Presently the Rabbi of Congregation Machzikei Hadas in Ottawa, Canada, Dr. Bulka is also the co-editor, with Joseph Fabry and William Sahakian, of the forthcoming volume *Logotherapy,* and author of *The Wit and Wisdom of the Talmud* (1974) and *Sex in the Talmud,* to be published this year.

JAN EHRENWALD received his M.D. degree from the University Clinic of Prague in 1925. A fellow of the Royal Society of Medicine and member of the Medico-Psychological Association, he is a diplomate of the American Board of Psychiatry, fellow of the American Psychiatric Association, fellow of the New York Academy of Medicine, and fellow of the American Institute for Psychotherapy and Psychoanalysis. Presently he is a Consulting Psychiatrist at the Roosevelt Hospital in New York City. His published work includes *Telepathy and Medical Psychology* (1948), *New Dimensions of Deep Analysis* (1955), *Psychotherapy: Myth and Method* (1966), and *History of Psychotherapy: From Healing Magic to Encounter* (1976), as well as more than 200 articles on neuropsychiatry, psychoanalysis, and parapsychology.

JAMES KIRSCH received his M.D. from Heidelberg University in 1923 and his American M.D. from New York University in 1943. He studied with C. G. Jung in 1929 and from then on remained in frequent contact with him until his death in 1961. He is founder of the Society of Jungian Analysts of Southern California and its past president. He maintains a private practice in Los Angeles and is the author of *Shakespeare's Royal Self* (1966) and *The Reluctant Prophet* (1973), as well as numerous articles. He is presently working on an extensive psychological study of Rabbi Nachman's stories and dreams.

NATHAN KUPERSTOK received his Ph.D. in clinical psychology from the University of Ottawa in 1977. His thesis investigated the effects of viewing media violence on aggressive behavior. He also studied at the Rabbinical College of Canada in Montreal. Formerly the co-director of the Biofeedback Training Clinic in Toronto, Kuperstok is now head of the Biofeedback Therapy Unit at the Keele Medical Centre North in Toronto.

JUDAH C. SAFIER received his M.S. degree from the University of Massachusetts in 1977 and is currently a doctoral candidate in the clinical psychology training program at that institution. Safier's research involves the ways in which a psychotherapist uses personal life history and experience in the service of another's growth. His own attempts to incorporate his background into his clinical work have led to a keen interest in the application of the Judaic perspective to psychotherapy. The present article is one of the fruits of this research.

ZALMAN M. SCHACHTER, ordained as Rabbi by Central Yeshiva Tomchei T'mimim Lubavitch in 1947, received an M.A. in Psychology of Religion from Boston University in 1956 and a D.H.L. from Hebrew Union College in Cincinnati in 1968. Formerly the head of the Department of Judaic Studies at the University of Manitoba, Dr. Schachter is presently Professor of Religion in Jewish Mysticism at Temple University. An acknowledged expert in the field of hasidic thought, Dr. Schachter has written extensively on this and other themes in leading journals and major books, and has also lectured as a visiting professor in leading universities. The present article is adapted from his major unpublished work on *The Yehidut: A Study of Counseling in Hasidism.*

MOSHE HaLEVI SPERO received his M.S.S.W. in psychiatric social work from Case Western Reserve University School of Applied Social Sciences and is a doctoral student in the Department of Social Work and Psychology, University of Michigan at Ann Arbor. Author of numerous essays on clinical and applied psychoanalysis in the *American Journal of Psychoanalysis, Journal of Jewish Communal Service, Judaism, Psychotherapy, Tradition,* and others, Spero is an associate editor of the *Journal of Psychology and Judaism.*

JONATHAN S. WOOCHER received his B.A. from Yale University in 1968 and his Ph.D. in Religion from Temple University in 1976. Dr. Woocher is Assistant Professor of Religion at Carleton College in Northfield, Minnesota, and has authored a study program on "Jewish Identity and Jewish Values," which is being published by the Council of Jewish Federations and Welfare Funds. Dr. Woocher is a member of the American Academy of Religion, the Society for the Scientific Study of Religion, and the Association for Jewish Studies. He is presently working a major study of "civil Judaism" in the United States, examining the religious symbols, values, and behaviors of the American Jewish polity.